# How to Stop Being

# Negative, Angry, and Mean

---

*Master Your Mind and Take Control*

*of Your Life*

**Richard Banks**

techniques outlined in this book.

# INTRODUCTION

*"Once you replace negative thoughts with positive ones, you'll start having positive results." – Willie Nelson*

All you have to do is look around the world and see that there is no shortage of negativity. This can make it extremely hard for a person who strives to be positive to make a positive impact on themselves and others. The truth of the matter is, we are all going to encounter negative circumstances and people throughout our lives. Unless we can learn how to manage these things effectively, we will forever remain prisoners in our lives instead of taking control of our own destiny. That's what this book is here to do.

Let me ask you something, how often over the last two weeks have you felt angry, out of control, or down? Hopefully, you haven't felt these things that often, but there is probably a good chance you have. If you hadn't, then you probably wouldn't be here right now. Just know, if these feelings are ever-present in your life, or at least feel as if they are, you are not alone. The good news is, those feelings can be transformed.

Everybody gets angry now and then, but some seem to stay angry, or at least get mad more often than others and lose control. This book will help you to get rid of that rage that often comes with anger. Additionally, this book will help people who are looking to have more control over their anger and emotions in general. These proven techniques can change your life forever. Just imagine not allowing your anger to take control of your life. When you use these techniques within the book, you will learn how to stop your anger in its tracks, and you will soon find that you are a much happier and positive person. You will know how to deal with your anger, instead of falling prey to it. You can use that energy to fulfill something in your life in a constructive way.

As an advocate for mental health, mindfulness, and positivity, I have scoured many studies and techniques and applied them to my own life, to figure out what helps and what doesn't. This, along with the years of experience, I truly understand the importance of mindset and psychology, and the role they play in achieving a person's goals and how they cope with disappointment, change, and stress.

This book is for people who have tried many other techniques and methods to control the anger and negative thinking but failed. This book will teach you how to set yourself free. You will discover the

11

reasons for your anger. Then you will find that those negative feelings lose the grip they have over you.

After reading through this book, you will find that you are more aware of the power you have always had. You will have steps that you can take to improve yourself, and skills to use to rewire your brain to reach a healthier mind. You will no longer be caught off-guard by the negative sides of life. Ultimately, What you THINK leads to how you FEEL, and What you FEEL leads to how you BEHAVE.

With my help and expertise, you will have the knowledge and skills you need to change your mindset and grow as a person. Now, I'm not telling you that the information I will provide you in this book is a magical cure-all pill for happiness, but it will help you to grow. This book is focused on helping you start your mental health journey.

The great thing is, is the brain is malleable and can

be changed. It also doesn't take a lot of tools to change the brain. All you need to do is be more aware of your internal dialogue and change it to something more positive and healthier. Why wait any longer? Let's get started and learn precisely how to be a more positive and happier person.

# CHAPTER 1: THOUGHTS VS. CORE BELIEFS

If you were to Google "thought," you are going to get a bunch of circular, uninformative information and definitions like "an idea or opinion produced by thinking or occurring suddenly in the mind." Merriam-Webster defines the word "think" as "to form or have in the mind." Neither of those definitions really tells us what a thought is.

When you have a thought, it represents something you have experienced. That representation is a likeness of the original experience. The representation that you have created in your mind has similar characteristics of the original experience. For example, a mold, imprint, image, or picture of an object is a representation of the original item.

## **Thoughts**

Thoughts are fundamentally just "maps" that correspond to a person's external environment.

Some scientists suggest that all thoughts are built upon analogy –making. The brain can detect similarities between new information and previous information, which enables the use of previously learned information to something new (Lewis, 2019).

People have automatic thoughts throughout the day as they make sense of what is going on. In a therapy setting, clients can get help to identify these automatic thoughts by asking things like:

- What do others say about this?

- What does this mean for you?

- What was going through your mind at that moment?

Some automatic thoughts have greater importance than others to understand what is going on in a person's mind. Recording these thoughts can give a person a better understanding of when automatic thoughts happen.

## Core Beliefs

A core belief is a central belief that a person holds about their self, the world, and others. Core beliefs tend to be formed early on in life and can refer to a cognitive construct like "I am unlovable" or "people can't be trusted." When a person feels anxious, it is common for the core belief "I am weak" to be activated. If they were in less threatening situations, the core belief "I am strong" could be activated. When they are activated, the person experiences

17

the beliefs as absolute truths.

There are times when people with depression or anxiety will develop strong core beliefs that aren't balanced through other core beliefs. In a therapy setting, one way to detect core beliefs is to notice thoughts that come along with a strong emotion that doesn't shift in the face of contrasting evidence (Lewis, 2019).

Let's look at an example:

Two students just took a test, and they both fail the test.

Person A's core belief is "I am a failure." Their reaction to this failed test would start with the thought, "Of course I failed... why bother?" This makes them feel depressed, and they don't do anything to change.

Person B's core belief is, "I am perfectly capable when I give my best effort." Their reaction to this failed test would start with the thought, "I did poorly because I didn't prepare." They would feel disappointed, and they would plan on studying harder before the next test.

One of the main challenges of changing your thought processes is being able to let them go. A possible explanation for this is that there could be a strong core belief at the root of that unhelpful thought. Core beliefs tend to be inflexible, rigid, and strongly-held beliefs that are maintained through the tendency to focus on the information that reinforced the belief and ignoring anything that contradicts it.

Not all core beliefs are inherently bad, but there is a good chance that you have some harmful core beliefs. These are those beliefs that are hidden beneath the surface-level. For example, a core

19

belief of "nobody likes me" could lie under the belief, "my friends only spend time with me out of pity."

Some other harmful core beliefs include:

- Helpless beliefs: "I am weak," "I'm a loser," "I am trapped."
- Unlovable beliefs: "I am unlovable," "I will end up alone," "No one likes me."
- Worthless beliefs: "I am bad," "I don't deserve to live," "I am worthless."
- External danger beliefs: "The world is dangerous," "People can't be trusted," "Nothing ever goes right."

These types of core beliefs have consequences. Mentally, they could cause low self-esteem, difficulty handling stress, substance abuse, anxiety, and depression. It can also affect your relationships, such as:

- Placing the needs of others before your own.
- Being overly aggressive or confrontational.
- Being overly jealous.
- Feeling inadequate in relationships.
- Difficulty trusting other people.

Since these core beliefs are learned, they can also be unlearned. Also, if the core belief is negative, there is a good chance that it is wrong, even if it feels right.

## **Perception**

*"A map is not the territory it represents, but, if correct, it has a similar structure to the territory, which accounts for its usefulness."* — Alfred Korzybski,

In the world of semantics, as stated by Alfred Korzybski, we have a world outside, and then we have five senses that we use to perceive the world.

We use our five senses to create a representation of the world, and that's how we see things. It is our internal representation of the world, which is different from everybody else's. This is what is called the map. The map is not the territory, just like your perception of the world is not the world (Marta, 2014).

If you are in a very emotional situation between you and somebody else, you have a perception of what's going on within you. You know who started it, who's to blame, but it may not be the same perception as the other person's. There could be a lot of drama, and your perception of it is not the actual situation. It's subjective.

The problem is, we often act as if the map is the territory. This is why we should have just enough self-doubt so that no matter what your reaction is, you realize it's still subjective. You understand that you could learn a little more about the situation. You

22

may recognize that the other person's point of view could be helpful. Maybe in the heat of the moment, when you are sure, you could stop and look at yourself and think about what is going on because your programming is involved.

We all want to make any relationship we have work, whether personal or professional, but the inferences that we make in certain situations tend to be inaccurate. Due to these inaccuracies, they cause us to act in ways that could be damaging to the relationship. It's important to keep the understanding that no matter what you think about a situation, it could be wrong.

Let's look at an example. If you saw a spider crawling up the wall right next to you, would you react? Most of you would say yes. This is what is known as the fight-or-flight reaction. Some people would run out of the room, and maybe some would try to fight the spider, but there is going to be some kind of reaction to it.

In this situation, the spider is the stressor, and you are the stressee. But, this is where perception comes into play. You realize that you didn't have your glasses on, and you take a second look and realize it was just a leaf. It only looked like a spider, but it wasn't one. In that sense, did the leaf cause you stress? Was the leaf the stressor? It was your perception that it was a spider that caused you to react.

Here's another example. People can get easily stressed out over time. They perceive their situation as if they don't have enough time to get everything done. They let the worry about time stress them out until they are frazzled, angry, anxious, or a whole host of other negative emotions. But you must learn to look at these things in a different light. Sure, some stress can help motivate you to get things done, but too much stress will hold you back. When simple

24

pressure that you have to get something done by its deadline turns into feelings of being overwhelmed, then it defeats its purpose as a motivator.

In this process of perception, there are three main parts. The first is the external event. This is the thing you are perceiving. It could be a person, a place, an object, or whatever else you experience. The second is the neural associations. When something on the outside happens to you, your brain makes neural associations with it. This is where you can say this happens, and then I react like this. You will start to notice reactive patterns. That's the third thing, your reactive frame. The reactive frame is how you frame the situation or how you experience it. These things happen automatically (Marta, 2014).

For example, if a person yells at you, your reaction to it could be to become indignant and upset with the person. But, if you take a step and reframe the situation, you could say, "They are having a bad day,

25

so it could be why they talked to me like that." You can also start thinking about what you can do to let them know you would rather them not talk to you in that tone of voice. If you are able to look at that person differently, you won't experience that physical reaction.

## Cognitive Distortions

"I just failed my math test. I'm not good at school. I might as well just drop out."

"I have the worst luck in the world."

"How do we know it would even work?"

"I'm not a creative person."

All of these are great examples of cognitive distortions. They are thought patterns that cause a person to view reality in an inaccurate way, which is usually negative. They are habitual errors in thinking. When you have cognitive distortion, the way you interpret something is usually negatively biased.

We all experience cognitive distortions at times. But when we end up reinforcing them regularly, they can increase anxiety, cause problems in relationships, deepen depression, and lead to many other issues.

Research has found that people develop these distortions as a way to cope with adverse life events. The more severe and prolonged those events are, the greater the odds are that one or more of these distortions are going to form. One of the earliest theories suggests that humans may have developed these distortions as an evolutionary survival method.

Stress can make a person adapt their thinking in ways that are helpful to their immediate survival. But most of these thoughts aren't healthy or rational long-term.

27

Researchers have found that there are at least ten common cognitive distortions.

1. Polarized Thinking

This is often referred to as black and white thinking. This distortion happens typically when a person habitually thinks in extremes. When you think that you are either going to succeed or doomed to fail, that people are either good or bad, you engage in this type of thinking.

2. Overgeneralization

When a person overgeneralizes, they conclude a single event, and then they incorrectly apply their conclusion towards everything. For example, they can make a bad grade on a test and conclude that they just suck in that class. They have a terrible experience in a relationship and assume all relationships are going to be like that.

### 3. Catastrophizing

This type of thinking causes a person to dread or assume the worst when they are facing something unknown. This causes ordinary worries to escalate quickly. For example, you don't get a check that you were expecting, and you catastrophize that you will never get it and that you won't be able to pay any of your bills, and your family will be evicted.

It's easy to dismiss this as an overreaction, but those who have developed this cognitive distortion might have experienced repeated adverse problems so often that they always fear the worst.

### 4. Personalization

This is the most common error in thinking, and that is taking things personally when they aren't even connected to you at all. This distortion can come up when you blame yourself for a situation that isn't your fault or was out of your control. Another example was when you incorrectly assume that you were intentionally targeted or excluded. It is often connected to depression or anxiety.

5.  Mind Reading

This is when people assume that they know what others are thinking. This can be hard to distinguish from empathy, which is the ability to understand and perceive what others feel. To spot the difference, it would be helpful to look at the evidence, and not just what confirms your beliefs.

6.  Mental Filtering

This is the tendency to ignore the positive and focus only on the negatives. When you interpret a circumstance with a negative filter, it is inaccurate and worsens depression and anxiety.

7.  Discounting Positives

Much like mental filters, this involved a negative bias in thinking. Instead of ignoring the positives, they explain them away as a fluke or luck. They don't acknowledge the good outcome as skill, determination, or a smart choice. They simply assume that it had to have been an accident or anomaly.

8.  Self-serving bias

This is the tendency to blame external forces when bad things happen and give yourself credit when good things happen. For example, when you win a poker hand, it is due to your skill at reading the other players and knowing the odds, while when you lose, it is due to getting dealt a poor hand.

9.  Confirmation bias

This is favoring information that conforms to your existing beliefs and discounting evidence that does not conform.

10. Labeling

This is a distortion where people reduce themselves or others to a single, negative descriptor, such as a failure or a drunk. Labeling can make a person berate. This misperception can cause some major problems between people.

The good news is that all of this can be fixed, and cognitive distortions can be eradicated.

**Recap**

Remember that your thoughts are created through the mix of stimuli and your core beliefs. While controlling your thoughts may difficult, it is not impossible. Your thoughts can change your life, so you must learn how to change your thought processes.

# CHAPTER 2: EMOTIONS

Emotions and thoughts are related, and we can experience them at the same time, but they are very different. Let's look a bit closer to see exactly what they are.

**Emotions**

It might help you if you think of emotions as an experience and flow of feelings like fear, anger, sadness, or joy. Emotions have an innate ability to be triggered by external or internal stimuli. External stimuli might be from watching a sad movie or seeing a friend suffer from a disease like cancer.

35

Internal stimuli might happen when you remember something sad.

Even though emotions are universal, everyone is going to experience and respond to them differently. Some might struggle with figuring out which emotion they are experiencing.

Emotions are there to help us connect with others and to help create strong bonds socially. People who can build strong emotional ties and bonds become part of a community and are more likely to find protection and support that is needed to survive.

People all over the world will have different thoughts, opinions, beliefs, and ideas, but most people will have the same feelings.

## **What Can Influence Our Emotions?**

Research has shown that emotions can be contagious. Humans have a tendency to mimic another person's outward state like when you pass someone in the grocery store, and they smile, you automatically smile back at them no matter what you might be feeling inward. Our outward state can affect our internal states, too, such as smiling could really make you feel happier.

Other factors that can influence emotions:

- Physical Conditions

Thyroid disorders, Alzheimer's, Multiple Sclerosis, Parkinson's Disease, strokes, brain tumors, and metabolic diseases like diabetes can cause someone's emotional responses to change drastically.

- Genetics

To get a bit more specific here, personality and brain structure, including one's self-control, can affect their emotional expression. Even though a person's genetics can't be changed, the brain is a completely different story. There are six definite "emotional styles" that get based on the structure of the brain, but we can reshape them with some practice.

- Cultural Beliefs and Traditions

These can affect how a person or group of people express their emotions. Some cultures deem it as "bad manners" if you express your emotions in ways that might not be considered appropriate and healthy in another culture.

## The Things We Think Can Impact the Things We Feel

Emotions and thoughts have a huge effect on each other. Our thoughts can trigger an emotion. It can also help you look at the emotion. Let's say you have a job interview in a couple of days, and you might begin feeling a bit scared. You can tell yourself that what you are feeling isn't a realistic fear.

Additionally, the way we appraise and attend to our lives can have an impact on the way we feel. If you have a fear of dogs, you will probably be a bit more attentive to the dog who lives across the street from you. You watch them very closely when they begin approaching you. You automatically start feeling threatened, and this can lead to some emotional distress. Someone else sees the dog coming, and the view them as being friendly, and they have an entirely different emotional response about the same situation.

## **Can Emotions and Thoughts Be Changed?**

We like believing that our emotions are just one more part of who we are, and they can't be changed. Research has shown that emotions are pliable. This means that they can be changed. Here are a few ways you can change them:

- By changing an external situation. For example, leaving an abusive partner.
- By changing your attention. For example, deciding to focus on a positive aspect of any given situation.
- By reframing the situation. For example, an upcoming test is an opportunity for you to learn and not an assessment of your worth.

The way you choose to live your life has massive power over how you feel each day. Specific kinds of mental training like positive thinking or mindfulness could affect how we look at the world and can help us feel happier, more resilient, and calmer. Other studies have found several other attitudes like kindness, gratitude, and forgiveness that can be practiced and cultivated (Lawson, n.d.).

## Defense Mechanisms

Defense mechanisms are behaviors that people use to remove themselves from unpleasant thoughts, actions, or events. These are psychological strategies that might help you put distance between yourself and the unwanted feelings or threats like shame or guilt.

Sigmund Freud first proposed the psychoanalytic theory, and it has evolved with time and says behaviors like defense mechanisms aren't under our control. Most people will do them without even realizing they are using them.

Defense mechanisms are a natural, normal part of

psychological development. Being able to identify the different types of defense mechanisms could help you with your future encounters and conversations.

There are several common defense mechanisms. Dozens have been found, but some get used a lot more than others. In many cases, these responses aren't under a person's control. This means you can't control "what you do when you do it." Here are the most common defense mechanisms:

- Denial

This is the most common defense mechanism. It happens when you won't accept facts or reality. You will block external circumstances or events from your mind so you won't have to deal with an emotional impact. You stay away from painful events or feelings.

This defense mechanism is the most widely one that is known, too. You will often hear the phrase: "They are in denial." This is understood to mean that a person is avoiding their reality despite what might be blatantly obvious to everyone else around them.

- Intellectualization

Any time you have been hit with a situation that is trying, you might decide to get rid of all the emotions from your responses and try to focus on just the facts. You might see someone use this strategy when someone loses a job, and they decide to spend their days making spreadsheets about leads and job opportunities.

- Compartmentalization

This happens when you separate your life into separate sectors. This might feel like you are protecting several elements about it.

Let's say you decided not to discuss your personal life at work, so you block off (compartmentalize) that part of your life. This lets you live your life without having to face the challenges or anxieties when you are in a specific mindset or setting.

- Reaction Formation

Anyone who uses this defense mechanism might see how they feel, but they decide to behave oppositely.

Anyone who reacts like this might feel they shouldn't ever express negative emotions like frustration or anger. Instead, they decide to respond in an extremely positive way.

- Sublimation or Redirection

This defense mechanism is thought of as a positive strategy. This is because the people who rely on it have decided to redirect their strong feelings or emotions into an activity or object that is safe and appropriate.

Rather than lashing out at an employee, you decide to funnel your frustration into exercise or kickboxing. You could also redirect or channel your feelings into sports, art, or music.

- Rationalization

Some people might try to explain their undesirable behaviors with a set of "facts." This lets them feel comfortable with the choice that they made, even if they know that it isn't right.

Let's say that a person gets turned down for a date. They may rationalize the situation by saying that they weren't attracted to the person anyway.

- Regression

If a person feels anxious or threatened, they might unconsciously "escape" into an earlier time in their life.

This kind of defense mechanism might be seen more in younger children. If they experience loss or trauma, they might act like they are young again. They might even start sucking their thumb or wetting the bed.

It can happen with Adults also. Adults who have a hard time coping with behaviors or events might start sleeping with a favorite stuffed animal, chewing on pens or pencils, chain-smoking, overeating comfort foods. They might stop doing their daily activities because they feel too overwhelming.

- Displacement

This is when you direct strong frustrations and

emotions toward an object or person that isn't threatening to you. This lets you satisfy your impulses to react, but you don't want to risk the consequences.

One good example is getting angry at your partner or child just because you had a rough day at work. Neither one is the cause of your strong emotions, but reacting to them won't bring as many repercussions as blowing up at your boss would.

- Projection

Some feelings or thoughts that you have about someone else might make you feel uncomfortable. If you project these feelings, you are misdirecting them to someone else.

For example, a bully may project their own feelings of vulnerability onto a smaller, weaker target.

47

- Repression

Irrational beliefs, painful memories, or unsavory thoughts might upset you. Rather than facing them, you might unconsciously decide to hide them, hoping you forget about them altogether.

This isn't saying that your memories are going to disappear. They might influence your behaviors, and they might impact your relationships in the future. You need to realize the impact that this defense mechanism is having on you.

## How to Be the Boss of Your Emotions

Being able to express and experience emotions is very important. As a response that is felt in any given situation, emotions can play a huge part in how you react. If you are in tune with them, you will have access to some critical knowledge that can help with:

48

- Self-care
- Daily interactions
- Successful relationships
- Making decisions

Even though emotions can help you with your life each day, they could hurt your interpersonal relationships and emotional health when they begin feeling out of control.

Any emotion, including positive ones, can be intensified until it becomes hard to control. With some practice, you can rein them in. Research has suggested that having the skills to regulate your emotions has been linked to our well being. They also found a possible link between financial success and these skills; working on that part might pay off literally.

Here are some suggestions to help you get started:

- Know When To Show Emotions

There is a time and place for everything, and this includes intense emotions. Uncontrollably sobbing is a normal response to losing someone you love. Punching and screaming into your pillow may help relieve some of your tension and anger when you get dumped.

Other situations need some restraint. It doesn't matter how frustrated you may be, screaming at your boss over cutting your hours isn't going to help.

You need to be mindful of where you are and the situation. This can help you know when it is fine to express your feelings or if you need to sit still and think about your feelings for some time.

- Breathe Deeply

There is a lot to be said for how powerful breath can be, whether you are so upset that you can't speak or if you are ridiculously happy. Slow down and pay attention to your breathing. Some deep breathing exercises could help you take a step back from the intense emotions and allow you to get grounded so you can avoid any extreme reactions.

The next time your emotions begin taking control:

- Inhale slowly; deep breaths will come from your diaphragm and not the chest. It might help you to imagine your breath coming up from deep inside your belly.
- Hold the breath for a three count and then exhale slowly.
- Think about a mantra. Some find that repeating a mantra can be helpful, something simple like: "I am relaxed." "I am calm."

- **Get Some Space**

Putting some distance between you and your feelings could help you react to them reasonably. This distance could be physical, like walking away from a situation that upset you. You could distract yourself by creating some mental distance.

You don't ever want to avoid or block your feelings completely, but it won't hurt you to distract yourself until you are in a place where you can deal with them better. Just be sure you come back to them. Any healthy distraction will just be temporary. You can try:

1. Spend time with your pet
2. Talk to someone you trust
3. Watch a funny video
4. Take a walk

- **Get Control of Your Stress**

If you are under a lot of stress, handling your emotions might be harder. People who are usually in control of their emotions might find it harder to handle them when they are under stress or a lot of tension.

Finding ways to manage your stress or reducing your stress might help you manage your emotions. Mindfulness practices such as meditation could help relieve stress, too. It isn't going to get rid of it entirely, but it could make it easier to deal with.

Here are some other ways to help you cope with stress:

1.  Take time to do your hobbies
2.  Take time to relax
3.  Spend time in nature
4.  Exercise
5.  Make time to laugh and talk with close friends

6. Get an adequate amount of sleep

- Meditate

If you already practice meditation, this might be your best method for handling your extreme feelings. Meditation helps you increase your awareness of all your experiences and emotions. While meditating, you will be teaching yourself how to sit still with those feelings. You will be able to see them without making them go away, trying to change them, or judging yourself.

Learning to accept your emotions can make regulating them easier. Meditation can help increase these acceptance skills. It offers you other benefits, too, such as helping you sleep better and relaxing you.

- Keep a Journal

Writing about your feelings and the responses that they trigger could help you to identify patterns. There are times when it might be enough to trace those emotions back through those thoughts. Putting your feelings onto paper can let you reflect on them on a deeper level.

It can help you see when certain circumstances contribute to emotions that are harder to control. Finding those triggers can make it possible to find ways to manage them better.

Journaling can give you the best benefits when you do it each day. Keep it with you and write down any intense feelings or emotions when they happen. Make sure you write down the triggers and then how you reacted to it. If the reaction didn't help, write in your journal to find things that will be more helpful for your future.

- Accept All of Your Emotions

If you want to manage your emotions better, you could try downplaying your feelings. If you tend to collapse to the floor sobbing and to scream when you can't find your keys, or you hyperventilate when you get good news, it might help you to tell yourself: "It isn't a big deal, so stop freaking out." or "Just calm down."

This won't work. It is invalidating your experience because, to you, it is a huge deal. Accepting your emotions as they come up helps you become comfortable with them. When you can increase your comfort level around these intense emotions, it will let you feel them entirely without reacting in unhelpful or extreme ways.

To practice accepting your emotions, you can try thinking about them as messengers. They aren't bad or good. They are only neutral. They might bring up some unpleasant feelings every now and then, but they are still giving you information that you can use.

You could try something like:

"I am upset because I keep losing my keys, and this makes me late. I should put a dish on the shelf by the door, so I remember to leave them in the same place."

When you accept your emotions, you will be able to find more positivity and fewer mental health problems. This can lead to more happiness over all.

- Identify Your Feelings

Take a few minutes to check in about your mood. This can help you gain control. Let's say you have been dating for a few months. You tried to plan a date last week, but they told you they didn't have the time. You texted them yesterday: "I'd like to see you soon. Can you meet this week?"

They respond 24 hours later: "Busy. Can't."

You get upset suddenly. Without thinking about what you are doing, you hurl your phone into the wall, knock over your trash can, and kick your chair, breaking your toe.

You can interrupt yourself by asking yourself these questions:

1. "What am I feeling right now?" furious, confused, or disappointed

2. "What happened to cause these feelings?" They ignored me without explaining why.

3. "Does this situation have a different explanation that makes sense?" They might have been stressed, sick, dealing with something that they don't want to explain to you. They may be planning on telling you more later.

4. "What do I want to do about these feelings?" throw things, scream, text them back something rude.

5. "Is there a better way to cope with them?" Ask them if everything is fine. Ask them the next time they will be free. Get some exercise.

When you think about all the possible alternatives, you will be reframing your thoughts. This can help you change your extreme reactions.

It might take some time before you can turn it into a habit. With some practice, doing these steps in your head will get easier.

- Stop Repressing Try to Regulate

Your emotions don't have a dial. But just imagine that you were able to manage your emotions by turning a dial. You wouldn't put them on maximum all day long. You wouldn't turn them completely off either.

Any time you repress or suppress your emotions, you are keeping yourself from expressing and experiencing these feelings. This might happen consciously or unconsciously. Consciously would be a suppressed emotion; unconsciously would be a repressed emotion.

Either one of these can lead to physical or mental health problems like:

- Substance abuse
- Difficulty managing stress
- Pain and muscle tension
- Sleep problems
- Depression
- Anxiety

When you are learning to gain control over your

emotions, be sure you aren't trying to sweep them under the rug. Healthily expressing your emotions involves finding a balance between no emotions and overwhelming emotions.

- Look at Your Emotional Impact

Having intense emotions isn't bad. Emotions can make your lives vibrant, unique, and exciting. Having strong feelings can show that we are embracing life fully, and we aren't suppressing normal reactions.

It is normal to experience some overwhelming feeling occasionally. If something great happens, if something terrible happens, if you feel like you have been missing out.

How will you know if there is a problem?

Any emotion that constantly gets out of hand could lead to:

61

- o Emotional or physical outbursts
- o Using illegal substances to manage emotions
- o Problems at school or work
- o Hard time relating to other people
- o Friendship or relationship conflicts

Take the time to figure out how your emotions are affecting your daily life. This makes it easier to find your problem areas.

- Find a Therapist

If you have tried all the above tips and your emotions are still overwhelming you, it might be time to find professional support. Persistent or long-term mood swings and not being able to regulate your emotions have been linked to specific mental health problems, including bipolar disorder and borderline personality disorder. Problems controlling your emotions could relate to family problems, trauma, or other problems.

A therapist can offer judgment-free and compassionate support while you:

- Practice reframing and challenging the feelings that cause you distress.
- Learn how to play limited emotional expressions up or downplay intense feelings.
- Address any severe mood swings
- Look at all the factors that contribute to your inability to regulate your emotions

Intense emotions and mood swings could provoke unwanted or negative thoughts that could eventually trigger feelings of despair or hopelessness.

This cycle might lead to unhelpful methods of

63

coping, such as self-harm or suicidal thoughts. If you start thinking about committing suicide, or have the urge to harm yourself, talk to someone you trust who could help you find some support immediately.

## **Recap**

You can't continue letting your emotions rule you. When you do, your emotions will dictate the things that you do, and that's going to end up causing you to miss out on things you want to do. Start identifying what you feel so that you can better understand your emotions. From there, try journaling or any of the other activities we have discussed. If you find that you can't get a grasp on your emotions on your own, get in touch with a therapist so that you can get the help that you need. Emotions are not easy to control, but always remember that you are not your emotions. You always have a choice.

# Chapter 3: Shifting Your Mindset

Why do some people shine in any circumstances that they decide to exert themselves, but other people can't manage a glimmer despite obvious talents? Research has shown that it is how they think about their abilities that count the most.

Most people who have reached greatness have worked very hard to get where they are. Most were told that wouldn't ever amount to anything, but they still believed in themselves and worked hard to accomplish it.

## **Growth vs. Fixed Mindset**

There are two different ways to look at ability or intelligence:

- Fixed Mindset: A person's ability and skills are ingrained or fixed. This means that we have been born with a specific ability level, and we won't ever be able to change it.

- Growth Mindset: We can develop our abilities through a lot of effort, hard work, and persistence. Persons with a Growth Mindset believe everyone can get better if they work at it.

The benefits of a growth mindset might seem obvious, but most of us are guilty of having a fixed mindset in certain situations. That can be dangerous because a fixed mindset can often prevent skill development and growth, which could sabotage your health and happiness down the line.

The varying beliefs can result in different behaviors, and ultimately different outcomes. Studies show that students who have a growth mindset can increase their grades with time; however, the ones who believed their intelligence was innate couldn't. Their grades actually got worse over time.

Believing that you are in complete control over your abilities can help you improve and learn. This is the true key to success.

Persistence, effort, and hard work are critical, but they aren't as important as believing that you are in complete control over your destiny.

People who have these mindsets will think differently and react differently to information. They will respond to information about their performance differently.

- People who have a fixed mindset, their brain will be the most active when they get information about how they performed, like on a test or their grades.

- People who have a growth mindset, their brain will be the most active while they are being told the things they can do to do better.

It is an extremely different approach from thinking, "How did I do?" to "What can I do better next time?"

The fixed mindset is more concerned about the results and the way they are looked at, and the growth mindset is more concerned about development and the ways they can improve. It should be obvious which one will lead to them having a better future.

## Handling Setbacks

Mindsets can cause people to handle their setbacks differently.

- People who have a growth mindset look at setbacks as a way to learn. They will generally try harder to overcome their problems.

- People who have a fixed mindset get discouraged by their setbacks since any setback will deplete how they view their abilities. They usually become disinterested and give up.

## Brain Plasticity

Do you realize that your brain can change? The old saying that "old dogs can't learn new tricks" isn't true.

69

The brain is very plastic. It can be molded and reshaped with time to form new pathways. This is why neuroscientists call this neuroplasticity. Neuroplasticity was once thought to occur only during childhood, but research in the latter half of the 20th century showed that many aspects of the brain can be altered even through adulthood.

These pathways get created by thinking or doing certain things. What we say or do can become hard-wired into our brains and turn into habits. These create routes that are very defined in our brains, and they become a part of our internal program. Neural plasticity is the ability of these pathways in the brain to change through growth and reorganization.

This is good news because now you know that you can change your mindset and your internal programming. The first step would be to realize that you need to be changed and then take the steps necessary to rewire your brain. You could view this

70

learning as a cycle to make it easier.

There are three things you can do to help create a growth mindset:

- You have to realize that having a growth mindset isn't just good; it is supported by science. This is saying that you have to be committed to creating a growth mindset.

- You can learn and then teach other people about the ways to improve and develop their abilities by adapting to a growth mindset. This can help you have control over your life. This can be very empowering. Science has shown that people who feel like they are in control of their lives usually perform better.

- Listen for a voice that is your fixed mindset. Anytime you hear a little, tiny critical voice in the back of your mind saying: "you can't do that," you can tell it to shut up that you can learn anything you want to.

## Using a Growth Mindset Throughout Life

Growth mindsets aren't just to help you learn new things. They can affect how we think about everything in life. A growth mindset could help you do better at work, in relationships, and sports.

Creating a growth mindset might just be the most important thing that you could ever do to help you get everything you want out of life.

## Are Certain People Smarter Than Others?

This can be answered with both "no" and "yes." When we are born, we have a genetic structure that is unique to us. This means that we are initially better than some people at various things. But, people who have developed a growth mindset believe that they can always catch up, improve, and move passed another's innate talents. This is the part where teachers help shape their student's outlook and confidence by giving them continuous, productive feedback. It is critical for teachers who understand the growth mindset do everything in their power to unlock that learning.

**Can We Share Mindsets?**

Sure. Humans can operate in both growth and fixed mindset. You might be wondering how we can operate in both growth and fixed mindset. Look at this example: Many people have a mindset that is fixed about jumping off a cliff. You hold no beliefs in being able to fly. You know you can't practice jumping off of a table or chair to be able to fly. Knowing you can't fly and you can't practice learning how to fly is an appropriate, normal fixed mindset.

When a person has a fixed mindset, they believe in their natural talent or intelligence as just fixed. They take time to document their talent or intelligence rather than developing them further. They believe that their talents are all they need to reach success. They don't think they need to put any additional effort into it.

If a person has a growth mindset, they think that they can develop their abilities with hard work and practice. Their talents and brains are just the beginning. By having this view, they can learn to love learning new things and have a resilience that is needed for great accomplishments.

Having a growth mindset is simply believing that you can develop your abilities and improve them through hard work and dedication. It isn't so much that these beliefs are magical. It is more the fact that without having a growth mindset, you won't exert the needed effort and you will stay stuck where you are at.

With a growth mindset, you can break through the "stickiness" and reach all the results that you desire. This might be moving up the corporate ladder, finding the love of your life, renewing your relationship with your partner, or any other aspect in your life.

Having a growth or fixed mindset can impact a student's learning experience from elementary school and into high school. Students who have a fixed mindset will give up if they can't figure out a problem. They will just admit defeat. This can damage their efforts in the future and could lead to limited growth. If they have a growth mindset, they will continuously try to improve their skills, and this can lead to more growth and then success.

**How to Know If You Have A Growth Mindset**

Do you think you were born with a particular set of abilities and skills, and these skills will stay with you for your whole life? For example, your IQ.

Do you believe any of the following about yourself?:

"It's hard for me to lose weight."

"I'm not good with numbers."

"I'm not an athlete."

"I'm not creative."

"I'm a procrastinator."

If you answered "yes," you have a fixed mindset, which will likely lead you to avoid experiences where you might feel like a failure.

Do you think that your beliefs and ideas are always changing, and you can learn new skills if you try, and

76

your intelligence and wisdom can grow with every unique experience?

If you answered "yes," you have a growth mindset.

It is okay if you have a fixed mindset. You can create a growth mindset. We will go over more about how to build it below.

**Why Does It Matter?**

The way we encourage and interact with our children can affect their attitude toward learning. Having a positive mindset makes the difference between a person giving up just because they aren't good at spelling and a determined struggle that brings growth. Having a growth mindset isn't all about effort. If a person has a fixed mindset, all they think about is the outcome. If they fail or they weren't the best, their effort was just wasted. For a person with a growth mindset, they value everything they do, no matter what the outcome. They tackle their problems, chart new courses, and work on important issues. They might not have found a cure for cancer, but they are still searching.

If you have a fixed mindset, you might shy away from challenges because you don't want to feel humiliated and embarrassed. Nobody does. This could be a problem due to a fear of making mistakes that could cause you to stay away from new experiences and challenges that might help you grow, improve yourself, and create a life you have always wanted.

If you have a growth mindset, you embrace facing challenges despite all the risks. This happens because you love growing and learning more than letting other people think you know what you are doing. Since you are always trying new things, you usually don't know exactly what you are doing. But those people who have a growth mindset usually build new skills easier because you believe you can, and you work hard at it.

Creating a growth mindset can help you have a fuller, more meaningful life since your life experiences will be a lot broader.

## Main Differences Between Growth and Fixed Mindsets

- Feedback and Mistakes

A person with a fixed mindset hates to make a mistake because they feel embarrassed. They might blame someone else or get defensive when criticized. A person with a growth mindset will view mistakes as a lesson they can learn from and won't take the criticism personally. When you are open to criticism, it can help you improve your ability to do better. This is just one more reason why having a growth mindset could bring you to success.

- Challenge

A person with a fixed mindset will stay away from challenges because they are afraid of failing and might hide just to avoid your responsibilities. A person with a growth mindset will find challenges engaging and exciting because they know they are going to learn valuable things from experience. They stay with the challenge, master it, and then they move on to bigger accomplishments.

- Effort

If a person with a fixed mindset is met with hard work, they might recruit other people to do the hard work or find an excuse to avoid it. They won't spend any effort to do what needs to be done. If a person with a growth mindset is met with hard work, they recognize that great accomplishments will require effort and persistence. Effort is a vital part of this process. If they want to master something new, they will have to apply a lot of energy, whether it be physical, mental, or repeating something over and over.

## Ways to Build Your Growth Mindset

Changing your mindset from being fixed to growth might seem hard to do, but if you take baby steps, if you want it bad enough, you can create a growth mindset.

Here is how you can do it:

- Realize and Embrace Your Imperfections

You need to be able to see and embrace all the imperfections in yourself and in others since it is the spice that makes us all unique. Everyone has flaws, deficiencies, and peculiarities. Just like the mole on Marilyn Monroe's face, imperfections make everyone unique.

- Bravely Face Your Challenges

If you realize that you are scared when faced with a challenge, stop and reframe the challenge in your mind. Think about your challenges as opportunities; by shifting your perspective just a bit, you will make it easier to engage with the challenge. Every challenge is an opportunity that is inviting us to experience new adventures.

Try various approaches to help coach yourself about ways to explore new paths or ways to create new skills, or ways to interact with new people, or ways to get through new circumstances. Fear is a feeling that we all can accept. You keep moving forward because it is new and exciting. If you can take this same attitude with a new challenge or a crisis at work, you might find new abilities that you never knew you possessed.

- Watch Your Thoughts and Words

Begin paying attention to what you say, even what you say in your mind. If your words are dark or low, it can cause the same results. You have to watch yourself; listen to everything you think and say. Begin censoring yourself and be your own guide.

You have to replace all negative thoughts with positive ones to create a growth mindset. Replace judgments with acceptance, hate with compassion, and doubt with confidence. If you disrespect yourself or lower your ethics, the outcome of these decisions and the consequences are going to reflect that. Have an intention to think better thoughts and keep yourself accountable.

- Quit Looking for Approval

When you look for approval from other people, it can keep us from developing a growth mindset. You have to cultivate your self-approval and self-acceptance. You have to learn how to trust yourself.

83

You are the only one who is always going to be there for you your whole life, so ultimately, you are the only person you should be trying to impress.

- Become More Authentic

When you pretend to be a person who you aren't will disrespect the true you. It shows that you are a fake. It lessens all that you have to offer. Becoming authentic is a process that is going to take a lot of time and work. When you do, you will be more driven to go after your goals, and this puts you in a growth mindset.

- Have a Sense of Purpose

Do you feel like you have a purpose in life? If you do, figure out what this purpose holds. If you just draw a blank, ask yourself what your life's purpose is until it gets clear. Think about or meditate on what your purpose may be. Sit for a few minutes until you

84

get a clear picture of what your life purpose is. Once you know what it is, make up your mind to pursue it. That will help you create your growth mindset.

- Rethink the Word Genius

Everyone has weaknesses and strengths. Identify and then appreciate your strengths and work on improving your weaknesses.

- Find Criticism's Gifts

The goal of constructive criticism is to coach and provide feedback. Other people can see what you are doing from a different perspective and might have some suggestions for you that can help you improve. It can be challenging to receive criticism from a co-worker, a peer, or someone that you don't fully respect, but it's important to remember that accurate and constructive feedback comes even from flawed sources. If you are open to hearing these suggestions and do not get defensive, you give yourself an opportunity for development and growth.

- The Process is Valuable

You need to value the process more than the result. It is the journey that matters and not the destination.

- Learn from Other People's Mistakes

If you have the ability the learn from other people's mistakes; you might be able to make fewer mistakes. This might lessen the fear when you are trying new things. This is the central aspect of creating your growth mindset.

- It is Okay to Say "Not Yet"

If you are struggling with something, remind yourself that it is okay; you just haven't mastered it "yet." If you just stick with it, practice and time are going to lead to improvement.

- Take Risks When You're with Others

Stop taking yourself so seriously. You need to be willing to make some mistakes in front of other people. If you are still growing, this is going to happen. The more often you embarrass yourself in front of others, the less it will bother you.

- Set Realistic Timelines

Acknowledge that it is going to take some time. It will take time to learn a new skill, such as playing an instrument or a new language. You might want to become a lawyer which is going to take a lot of time. Remember that being realistic can help you with your growth mindset.

- Speed Isn't Important

If you have a growth mindset, your end results won't matter. You will completely engage and put in all the effort that it is going to take, and it won't matter how long it takes you to get the results. When you focus on the process, it will usually improve the results since you put in a lot of effort on the way.

- It's Your Attitude, Own It

If you want to have a growth mindset, you have to take the time and make an effort to create it. If you persist, opportunities will come your way. You will be pursuing resilience on your way. You are remolding your mind, and that is a great thing.

**<u>Recap</u>**

When you have a growth mindset, it means that you are embracing challenges, persisting when you face any setbacks, taking responsibility for your actions and words, and acknowledging all the effort on the path toward success. This is the reason why "practice makes perfect."

When you choose to take extra efforts to create your growth mindset, you will be able to make all your mental processes work for you. This can result in a large possibility that you will get the results that you are looking for and you will be able to live the life that you want.

# CHAPTER 4: UNDERSTANDING NEGATIVITY

We all engage in negative thinking now and then, but constant negativity will destroy your mental health, causing you to feel anxious and depressed. Science has found that positive thinking can improve our mental wellbeing, lower our stress levels, and lead to better cardiovascular health. Yet, most of us get stuck in negative thought patterns. Let's explore the world of negative thinking.

## What Counts as a Negative Thought?

If you analyze your thoughts, it can be difficult to

differentiate negative thinking from simple worries that everybody has. Feeling sad about something that is upsetting is normal, just like it's normal to worry about relationship troubles or financial burdens. But it is when those feelings become pervasive and repetitive that problems show up.

Negative thinking is when you have a negative view of yourself and your surroundings. While most people will experience negative thoughts, negative thinking that seriously affects the way you view yourself and the world around, and even interferes with your life, could be a sign of mental illness.

Not everybody who experiences negative thinking will have a mental illness, just like not everybody who has a mental illness suffers from constant negative thoughts. That said, negative thinking can seriously hurt your quality of life and mental health, especially if you aren't able to stop it. Luckily, there are ways to bring those thoughts to an end, but you have first to know what causes them.

## **Negativity Bias**

We've all been there when we catch ourselves dwelling on a mistake. Criticism tends to affect us a lot more than compliments, and bad news always gets more attention. The reason this happens is negative events simply have a more significant impact than positive ones. This is what psychologists call a negativity bias. This bias can have a massive effect on our actions, decisions, and relationships.

Negativity bias is our tendency to register negative things more often than we do positive things, as well as to dwell on those things. This causes us to feel the pain of rejection more than we would feel the joy of praise (Maloney, 2020).

This is the reason why bad first impressions can be

93

so hard to overcome and why our previous traumas can linger for so long. In pretty much every interaction we have, there's a greater chance of noticing negative things and remembering them more vividly later on.

We all tend to:

- Respond strongly to negative events.
- Remember negative things more often than positive ones.
- React in a strong way to negative stimuli.
- Recall the insults we have received rather than praise.
- Remember our traumatic experiences more vividly.

For example, you could be having an amazing time at a family get-together when one of your relatives makes an offhand comment that irritates you. You start to notice that you are stewing over what they said for the rest of the party. Once you get home, and somebody mentions the party, you reply about how horrible it was, even though, for the most part, it was a good party.

Research has found that this negative bias will also influence our motivation to finish a task. People are more motivated if something they desire is going to be taken away as opposed if the incentive is to give them something.

This can play a significant role in your motivation to reach your goals. Instead of focusing on the things that you are going to gain, you may want to focus on what you are going to lose if you don't reach that goal.

Other studies have also found that people assume that negative news is always the truth. Since negative information will draw people's attention more, it can be seen as having more validity. This is likely why bad news tends to get more attention.

This negative tendency is likely due to an evolutionary process. Earlier in human history, noticing dangerous, harmful, or negative threats in the world was a matter of life and death. Those who paid more attention to danger were more likely to live. This means that they were also more likely to hand down the genes that made them more attentive to danger.

Neuroscience has found that there is more neural processing within the brain when it comes to negative stimuli. Psychologist John Cacioppo conducted studies where he showed participants pictures that were either neutral, positive, or negative and observed the electrical activity within their brain. He found that there was a stronger response within the cerebral cortex when they saw negative images than when they viewed neutral or positive ones (Maloney, 2020).

96

## **What Causes Negative Thoughts?**

There are many different causes of negative thinking. Intrusive negative thoughts may be a sign of generalized anxiety disorder, OCD, depression, or some other mental health condition. While negative thoughts can signal a possible mental health problem, it can also simply be a part of life and your internal programming. Since these negative thoughts can affect you so much, you should learn what is causing them.

There are three leading causes of negative thoughts.

1. Fear of the Future

People tend to fear the unknown and don't know what the future may hold. This can cause a person to start catastrophizing, which means they think the future is going to be a disaster. Whichever way you see it, worrying about what the future holds is just a waste of energy. The key to releasing these negative thoughts is to accept that you cannot predict the future, and it's more rewarding to focus on the present.

2. Anxiety about the Present

It's understandable to be anxious about the present. Many of us worry about how others feel about us, if we are doing well at work, and how long we will be stuck in traffic during our commute. Negative thinking, on the other hand, will come up with the worst-case scenario. They think nobody at work likes them, and the boss is about to tell them they are the worst employee, which is going to make them late to pick up their kids from school. Again, all of this comes from the fear of losing control. Routine and organization can help get rid of some of these negative thoughts, but you might also find help through practical therapy techniques.

3. Shame about the Past

Have you ever laid awake in bed worrying about something you did yesterday, last week, or last year? Everyone has had disappointing moments at some point, but negative thinkers will often dwell on past failures and mistakes much more than other people will. Of course, a better approach would be to accept that they happened and think about how you could prevent it from occurring again in the future.

## Why Can't They Just Stop?

For anybody who suffers from intrusive negative thoughts, hearing somebody say, "Why can't you just be happy" makes you feel hopeless, angry, or any other negative emotion. The thing is, you want to feel happier. Nobody wants to be stuck in those negative thoughts, but they are hard to stop. It's important to point out - if you do suffer from

99

negative thoughts, it does not make you a bad person, no matter what other people may say to you.

There is a reason why these negative thoughts are hard to get rid of. Negative thoughts are like a train wreck; you don't want to look, but you just can't look away. While it may be dreadful to see, it is also exhilarating.

This enticement happens when the brain releases reward chemicals, like dopamine. Since we receive a reward for those thoughts, they get repeated over and over again until they become habitual. Within the brain, we form these habits in the basal ganglia, which is the oldest and most primitive part of our brain. This is what scientists call the "lizard brain."

Since we form habits in such a primitive area of the brain, they pretty much get hardwired in. They have such deep roots in our brain; some scientists believe that habits can't be destroyed and can only be replaced by new ones. For example, a person may smoke to have a break from their workday. When you feel bored, you choose to go outside a chew a piece of gum instead. When you do this enough times, the habit of smoking will be replaced with the habit of chewing gum.

The issue here is that negative thoughts aren't just a habit. When the brain believes that some bad is also beneficial, it turns into an addiction. In most cases, when a person replaces an addiction, it gets replaced with something that's equally, if not more, dangerous, like drugs or drinking. While this sounds very hopeless, there is hope; continue reading.

## Types of Negativity

Negative thoughts and negativity can show up in many different ways, most of which you will likely be familiar with.

101

1.  Cynicism

This is where a person has a general distrust of people and their motives.

2.  Hostility

This is where a person is unfriendly to others, and they are unwilling to create a healthy relationship.

3.  Filtering

This is where a person notices only the bad in what should be a happy moment.

4.  Polarized Thinking

This is a belief that if someone or something isn't perfect, then it has to be horrible.

5.  Jumping to Conclusions

This is where a person assumes something terrible is going to happen because of their present circumstances.

6. Catastrophizing

This is the belief that disaster is inevitable.

7. Blaming

This is where a person blames others for personal problems and feel as if they are the victim of the uncontrollable events of life.

8. Emotional Reasoning

This is where a person uses their emotions to define what is real and what isn't.

9. Fallacy of Change

This is a thought process where if a person or

circumstance changes, you will then be happy.

10. Heaven's Reward Fallacy

This is a type of negativity where a person assumes that there is always going to be a reward for sacrifice and hard work. When they don't get the reward, they become depressed and bitter.

## **The Dangers of Negative Thoughts**

Once your negative thoughts move from normal, given the circumstances, into intrusive and constant, you are opening yourself up to many dangers. Constant negative thoughts can cause mood disorders, high blood pressure, depression, and chronic anxiety.

Physically, negativity can show up in the form of:

- Drastic metabolism changes

- Sleep problems
- Upset stomach
- Fatigue
- Chest pains
- Headache

Mentally, negativity can show up in the form of:

- Social withdrawal
- Depression
- Anxiety
- Schizophrenia
- Personality disorders

The reason why constant negative thoughts can have such a negative effect on not just your mind but your body as well is that it causes chronic stress. This stress upsets your hormonal balance, damages the immunes system, and depletes the brain of chemicals needed for happiness. Chronic stress can decrease lifespan.

For example, hostility, or anger, if poorly managed or repressed, can cause a slew of health problems, like high blood pressure, infections, digestive disorders, and cardiovascular disease.

Let's look at what cynicism can do. A 2014 study by the American Academy of Neurology connected high levels of cynicism later in life to a higher risk of dementia when compared to those who were more trusting. This was even after taking into account other risk factors like smoking, certain heart health markers, sex, and age.

Our emotions and thoughts have widespread effects on how our body works, such as immune function, hormone release, and metabolism. Plus, there is the fact that when somebody is feeling down, they are more likely to take part in drinking or smoking or other unhealthy habits.

## **Negativity in Relationships**

Beyond just the personal effects of negativity, it can affect your relationships as well, especially those of the romantic kind. We know how a negativity bias causes us to focus on the bad, more so than the good. Well, think about how that works in a relationship. Negativity holds up a magnifying glass to your partner's faults, whether real or imagined. You are also biased by your own confidence that magnifies your strengths. You start to wonder how your partner could possibly be so selfish and blind to all of your virtues and everything you have done for them. You start asking, why don't they appreciate me?

Psychologists have found, by asking couples to rate their satisfaction in the relationship, that things typically decline over time. They also found that the most successful marriages are defined not by improvement, but by avoiding that decline. This

107

doesn't mean marriage is hopeless, but that initial thrill of infatuation is going to fade, and that's why couples have to find other sources of contentment. But there are times when this decline in satisfaction is so steep that it dooms the marriage.

Let's look at a scenario. Your partner does something that annoys you. It could be anything from spending too much, ignoring you while you talk, or flirting with your friends. How will you respond?

1. Let it go and hope it gets better.

2. Explain what is bothering you and work out a compromise.

3. Sulk. Don't speak up, but emotionally pull away from them.

4.  Head for the door. Threaten to leave them or start looking for someone new.

In one study, psychologists identified two basic strategies that couples use when faced with these types of problems, constructive and destructive. Each of these strategies could be active or passive.

The constructive strategies were admirable and didn't make much of a difference in the relationship long-term. Remaining passively loyal, as in the first response, didn't have a significant impact on the relationship, and actively trying to reach a solution, as in the second response, only helped things a little.

What was more intriguing was the results of the destructive strategies. If you start to withdraw silently, as in the third response, or you get angry and throw around threats, as in the fourth, you can create a disastrous spiral of retaliation. When this happens, it creates a significant strain on the relationship. The negativity has taken over, and it's hard to overcome it. That's why it is so important to learn how to identify and control your negative bias, so it isn't able to take hold of your life or your relationships.

## Working Through Three Common Negative Thinking Patterns

It can be difficult to identify negative thinking patterns, mainly because our thoughts feel so true. We tend to accept them uncritically and don't question them. We are going to look at three common negative thought patterns and how you can change them to something healthier.

1. Negative Rumination

While this natural and can be a healthy way to self-reflect, reflection ends up becoming a problem when it is repetitive, negative, and excessive.

Rumination is a negative thinking pattern where you get mentally stuck and continue to spin your wheels without moving forward at all, like a car stuck in the mud. Rumination can end up making you feel more anxious as you continue to stew on the negative outcomes that may happen.

When you notice yourself ruminating, do something to change your thoughts up. Try taking a walking or talking to a friend. Make sure, though, if you choose to talk, don't start talking about what you were ruminating over.

2. Overthinking

Overthinking happens when you start to process different options over and over, trying to figure out all possible outcomes and everything that might occur in the future, to make sure you make the best choice. The problem with this is that you attempt to try to control something that you can't control.

There is no way to predict the future. With every choice, there is going to be an unknown.

What you should do is limit the time you spend thinking about the decisions you need to make before acting. Make a deadline as to when the decision needs to be made, even if it doesn't feel comfortable. Only give yourself the chance to research a few alternative options, not every single one.

3. Cynical Hostility

This is a way of thinking and reacting that is marked by angry mistrust of others. You view people as threats. You think that they may deceive you, let you down, take advantage of you, cheat on you, or otherwise cause you harm. Cynical hostility means you interpret other people's behavior in the worst way. You may believe that a driver in front of you is deliberately driving slow to make you mad or that your friends have some ulterior motive.

What you should do instead is try to get a bit of distance between you and the judging thoughts. Notice when you start to think in a distrustful way, and deliberately think of other ways to view the situations. What is something that could be motivating a person's actions that are benevolent or less toxic? Learn to reserve your judgments and look for actual evidence before you label a person. Notice how your own actions can push people away or prompt them to react negatively towards you.

## Other Ways to Overcome Negativity

Negative thoughts can appear in many different ways, so it's important to be prepared for any negative thoughts that may arise. We will finish out this chapter by looking at some other ways to train yourself to stop having so many negative thoughts.

1.  Schedule Your Negative Thoughts

This may seem paradoxical, but you can gain control over your negative thoughts by scheduling ten minutes a day to ruminate and review those negative thoughts. If you experience a negative thought during the day, write it down, and tell yourself that you will review it during your NTT (Negative Thought Time). The NTT has to be every day and can only last ten minutes. Over time, you will start to gain control over your negative thoughts.

2.  Replacing the Negative Thought

Getting rid of the negative thoughts usually is easier to do if you simply replace it with a positive thought. This can be done in four steps. First, notice when you start the pattern. Second, acknowledge that it is a pattern you want to get rid of. Three, articulate what you would like to do differently. Four, choose

114

a different behavior that is going to serve your goal.

3. Write It Down

Write down the reason for your negative thoughts. Writing things down, versus thinking about them, helps to purge the thought, and when you see it on paper, it makes it easier to understand it.

4. Ask Tough Questions

Take some time to reflect on your answers to these questions:

- What do these negative thought patterns give you?
- What do I lose when I engage in these negative thoughts?
- What benefits would I have if I engaged in positive thoughts?

- What happened in my past that has caused me to be negative?
- What will I do now?

5. Give Up the Morning News

Research has found that only three minutes of negative news in the morning will increase the odds of a negative experience during the day. Research has also found that a positive mindset can increase satisfaction and productivity.

**Recap**

Negative thinking can't be avoided altogether, but it can be controlled. Allowing your negative thoughts to become compulsive and uncontrollable, you are risking the damaging side effects of these thoughts. Start taking note of the times that you think negatively, and then learn how to keep them at bay. Schedule your negative time so that it doesn't consume your entire day.

# CHAPTER 5: UNDERSTANDING ANGER

What exactly is anger? It is one of our basic emotions. It is just as elemental as disgust, anxiety, sadness, or happiness. All of our emotions are tied to our survival, and we have been honed throughout history. Anger is a close relative to the freeze, flight, or fight response. It gets us ready to fight. Fighting doesn't have to mean hitting someone; it may motivate a community to take on some form of injustice by enforcing new behaviors or changing a law or two.

If you get angry too often or too easily, it can harm your relationships, and it could be harmful to your body. Having too many stress hormones released into the body can destroy neurons in the brain that is associated with short-term memory and judgment. It can also weaken your immune system.

## How to Control Anger

Everybody has felt that feeling. It's the rage that comes up when someone cuts you off on the road. You just want to push the gas pedal to the floor and make an obscene gesture to them. Anger won't go away just because you express it. This can actually deepen and reinforce it.

Just like any other emotion, anger needs to be driven through self-awareness, so it won't erupt into violent, aggressive, or hostile behaviors toward other people or causes you to harm yourself. Most cities have support groups that help you manage your anger. These can either be in individual or group settings. Cognitive restructuring might also help because they help the patient to reframe their inflammatory and unhealthy thoughts.

## When Does Anger Become a Disorder?

Everybody is going to feel angry at some point in their lives. It becomes a problem when the severity or frequency of your anger interferes with your mental health, legal standing, performance at work, or relationships. Even though there isn't an official "anger disorder," dysfunctional anger is a symptom of manic episodes, "intermittent explosive disorder," and "borderline personality disorder." You don't need a formal diagnosis for anger to get disruptive or to get help managing it.

## What Causes Anger

There are nine main reasons anger can occur:

1.  Unmet Needs or A Threat to Safety

Maslow came up with a hierarchy of needs. These are things that a person requires to feel safe and happy in their life. Before anybody can deal with the needs high up on the pyramid, their basic needs have to be met. These basic needs include food, water, warmth, rest, security, and safety. When those basic needs aren't satisfied, we can experience anger.

This anger results from the fact that we have to start fighting for those needs. The longer the deprivation lasts, the more motivated we are to fulfill those needs. For example, the longer a person is without food, the hungrier they become. We become willing to fight for these needs to be met. If these needs aren't satisfied, then our body is unable to function optimally.

2. Grief and Loss

When we lose someone that we were close to, we

122

go through five stages of grief. This includes denial, anger, bargaining, depression, and acceptance. To move to the next stage, you have to work through the present, but why do we get angry?

Becoming angry during grief is connected to the previous cause of anger. Our basic human needs are threatened. Then you add in the other changes that happen after the death of a loved one. It could cause a change of location, financial status, family relations, and more. This anger can show up in many different ways. You could be angry at the love who died. You could be angry with your higher power for taking your loved one. You could be angry at the disease that took them. Often, it is easier to express anger than try to figure out why we are really upset.

3. Boundaries are Violated

Healthy individuals have boundaries. Boundaries protect us from being taken advantage of or being

123

run too thin. They are beneficial to have, and all individuals should create boundaries. That said, sometimes those boundaries get violated. When that happens, we may respond with anger. Anger is pretty intense, so chances are if you do get angry at a person for your boundary violation, then they have likely been ignoring your boundaries for a while.

In a sense, when they ignore your boundaries, they are disrespecting you, telling you that your feelings don't matter and that they are trying to control you. This is why we end up angry at those people.

### 4. Disappointment and Shattered Expectations

We hate to be disappointed, whether in ourselves or others. To feel disappointed means that something has let you down. Things didn't go as planned, or a person didn't act as you had hoped they would. When something always disappoints you, it can end up causing you to feel angry. This ties back into the

124

first point of our basic needs, especially if it has to do with a person in our life that we see as a parental figure. We are supposed to be able to rely on them, but if we can't, we think we have lost our security. Thus, feelings of disappointment and anger arise.

5.  Guilt and Shame-Based Identity

Anger can be used to cover up guilt and shame. This is because we react defensively when we get criticized or even get mild feedback. This means we use anger to divert attention away from the pain.

6.  Unforgiveness – Bitterness, Resentment, and Revenge

Bitterness, resentment, and revenge are low-grade anger responses. A perception of unfairness triggers these emotions. If somebody didn't praise you when you thought they should, you might feel resentful. The problem is, we often stick with these emotions. We don't forgive the person we believe wronged us, and this low-grade anger response starts to build into full-blown anger. Sometimes by the time, it reaches ahead, we have forgotten what caused us to get upset in the first place.

### 7. Vitamin Deficiency

While this may sound weird, a deficiency in B vitamins can be an underlying cause of anger. B vitamins are connected to preserving brain health. B1 and B5 specifically lead to symptoms of irritability. Having a B vitamin deficiency is often caused by a lack of micronutrients in your diet.

### 8. Substance Abuse

Substance abuse and anger are two sides of a coin. Often, a person will have anger before they start abusing drugs or alcohol. They get so consumed in their rage; they are willing to try anything to put an end to it, so they turn to substances to try and numb the anger. The problem here is, the substance typically causes feelings of anger to become stronger and harder to control.

9.  Unresolved Childhood Distress

Unresolved childhood trauma can cause many different issues in adulthood. One of which is anger. If you grew up in a household where anger was expressed in an unhealthy manner, you might think anger is bad. That means you start to suppress the anger because you don't know how to use it correctly. The problem is, you are still angry, but that anger continues to build until it comes out in an unhealthy way.

## Everybody Has Triggers

There are several ways our brains can get triggered. These triggers will be different for everybody based on their life experiences. For example, if you were bullied a lot when you were younger, your triggers are going to be very intense towards a person who is threatening or controlling.

Here are some of the most common anger triggers:

- Certain people or personalities
- Not having enough control
- Being disappointed constantly
- Disputes within a relationship
- Lying
- Misinformation
- Insults
- Physical threats
- Blaming
- Shaming
- Labeling
- Abusive language
- Violating your personal space
- Disrespect

- Injustice

Any of these triggers can cause somebody to experience a total amygdala breakdown. Adults who had volatile experiences during childhood could get extremely angry if those situations get recreated in their adult lives.

We have to know what triggers our anger and to be aware of the problems that put our brains on high alert and might send us over the edge. When we have found our triggers, it will help us to determine why they cause this kind of response.

It can be helpful to write down your triggers as you start to recognize them. By doing this, you will prepare yourself for an outburst.

**<u>Anticipating Your Anger</u>**

Knowing the reasons for your triggers will help you

129

anticipate an outburst. When you know your triggers, you will be able to take control of your anger. You will be keeping the process inside the cortex rather than in the limbic system. You will be able to give a deliberate response that will quiet the outburst.

If you are aware and in tune with your triggers, then you will be able to predict your response and make a choice not to respond angrily. This means that you will be:

- Able to see what is happening around you that caused the trigger, and

- Take any measure necessary to talk yourself into a better response that allows you to handle the way you are reacting.

When you are in charge of your reactions, this comes from maintaining self-control because you know what is happening within your brain, and you know your triggers. Your emotions and thoughts stay in your cortex, where you will be able to be less emotional and more strategic.

## **Tips to Help You Control Your Anger**

Controlling your anger is essential to help you stay away from doing or saying something that you might regret. Before your anger gets out of control, you can use some of the following strategies to help you control it:

- Get Creative

Turn anger into a project. Think about writing a poem, work in the garden, or pain when you get upset. Emotions can be a delightful muse for creative people. Use it to help lessen your anger.

- Express It

It is OK to express the way you feel if you handle it correctly. Ask a friend that you trust to help you be accountable. Outbursts won't solve anything, but talking maturely could help you not feel as angry or stressed. It could prevent problems in your future.

- Have Empathy

Try walking in someone else's shoes and look at the situation from their perspective. If you can relive the events or tell the story from their point of view, you might gain a better understanding and be less angry.

- Write the Person

Write an email or letter to whoever made you feel angry. DON'T send it. Delete it. Most of the time, just expressing your emotions in some way is all you need, even if it is something that won't be seen by anyone other than you.

- Laugh

Nothing can get rid of a bad mood, like getting into a good one. Get rid of your anger by finding ways to laugh. It might be scrolling through some memes, watching your favorite comedian, or playing with your children.

- Change Up Your Routine

If just thinking about your commute to work gets you angry before you have had your morning coffee, try to find a new route to work. Think about options that might take more time but won't leave you frustrated and upset.

- Pause and Go Over Your Response

You can stop an outburst by first pausing for a moment and going over what you will say or the way you were going to approach the problem. This time will give you all the time you need to play out several solutions.

- Find an Immediate Solution

You may be angry that your child left their toys thrown all over their room before they went to a friend's house. Close their door. You can put a temporary end to your anger just by getting it out of your sight. Look for similar resolutions for all other situations, no matter how subtle it may seem.

- Journal About It

All the things that you can't say to a person, maybe you can write about it. Write down all the things you are feeling and ways you would like to respond to them. Processing them through writing could help you calm down and look at the events that brought you to what you are feeling in this present moment.

- Take Some Action

You can harness your angry energy by doing something productive. Write a letter to your congressman, mayor, or whomever about some law that needs to be changed. Do something nice for somebody who lives close to you. If you have elderly neighbors, check and see if they need any help. Pour all those emotions and energy into something productive and healthy.

- Give Yourself a Time Out

Take a break. Sit by yourself. During this quiet time, you will be able to process all the events and get your emotions back to normal. You might even realize that this time by yourself is very helpful, and you want to do this on a daily basis.

- Listen to Music

I've always heard the old saying of: "Music calms the savage beast." Allow the music to carry you far away from what you are feeling. Go to your car or put on some headphones. Tune into your favorite music and dance, bop, hum, or sing your anger away.

- Escape Mentally

Find a quiet place, close your eyes, and just imagine yourself relaxing in your favorite vacation spot. Notice every detail of this imaginary place: What is around you? Do you hear water running? Are you on a sandy beach? Is there a breeze blowing? This can help you find peace in the middle of anger.

- Go for a Walk

Exercise has been known to help reduce anger and calm the nerves. Take a walk, ride your bike, or hit the gym. Anything that gets you moving and your heart pumping is good for the body and mind.

- Count

It doesn't matter which way you count. It can be up or down in increments of ten. If you are outraged, begin at 100 or go to 100. In the time it takes you to count, your heart rate will slow down, and your anger will disappear.

## Suppressing Your Emotions

It isn't just long-term health that might suffer if you continuously suppress your emotions. There have been many studies that have shown when we ignore or mismanage our emotions, it can create short-term physical and mental deficiencies.

When you suppress your emotions, whether it is frustration, grief, sadness, or anger, it could cause lots of physical stress on the body. The effects will be the same, even if the emotions are different. It could affect your self-esteem, memory, and blood pressure.

If you suppress your emotions for a long time, you have a more considerable risk of heart disease and diabetes. Neglecting your emotions could lead to problems with depression, anxiety, aggression, and memory.

When you don't acknowledge your emotions, you are just making them stronger. For example, you may be angry at your sister, and after you have sat and stewed in this anger, but still didn't say anything, you are encouraging an outburst.

A few weeks have passed, and you are going to work, a car cuts you off, you immediately go into full-blown road rage and hit them, causing a huge accident. That overreaction and explosion of emotions to this situation was your body's way of releasing all those pent-up emotions.

## Handling Strong Emotions

Learning the right way to handle your emotions is hard. There are some steps you can take if you are feeling overly emotional and don't know how to handle it.

- Take Time to Take Care of Yourself

Any kind of activity that allows you to take care of yourself, relaxes you, or calms you down can be beneficial. Studies show that exercise can help with emotional stress. If you are experiencing some challenging emotions, you can regulate them by doing meditation, some aerobic exercises, or you could practice gratitude and forgiveness toward the person or situation.

- Own Your Response

To know what you are feeling, you need to think

about the way you dealt and reacted to the situation. Take some time to really think about what got you to where you are at. Now think about ways you can keep that from happening in the future. If it is something that can't be avoided, like grief, think about it and ways you can handle it better using some of the tips provided previously.

- Confront It

If you can, confront the situation or person that is triggering your emotion with a goal in mind of resolving that problem. If you can't do this, learn how to "observe" the situation to empower yourself.

When you "observe," you are taking yourself out of the problem and not taking the situation personally. Look at the situation as if you aren't a part of it. Calmly figure out what the other person was feeling or thinking and what could have made them act a specific way.

140

When you observe a situation, it allows you to learn more about a person instead of getting frustrated, angry, or taking their actions personally. If you can't confront the problem, talking to someone you trust can lessen the emotion and could have therapeutic effects on your brain.

- Acknowledge Your Emotions

Realizing that you are feeling a certain way is very important. You don't need to do this out loud; you can do this internally. You might think you are feeling angry, but it might be something more complex. You might be feeling sad, but you revert to anger because it is an emotion you are more comfortable with.

You need to find and understand the core emotion behind your feelings. Take the time to answer these questions:

    o   "Why am I feeling this reaction?"

    o   "Why am I acting this way?"

Just finding and describing the feeling could have beneficial effects.

## **Recap**

Anger is a rational emotion in certain situations. We can't continue to make people suppress their anger just because we are afraid of the emotion. The first thing you need to do is learn your triggers. Once you recognize your triggers, you can start doing what you need to do to express your anger healthily and safely.

# Chapter 6: Understanding Pessimism

The clouds in the sky never seen to have a silver lining, and your glass is half empty. Pessimists take a lot of crap because of their negativity and always expecting the worst in everything.

Other than taking a toll on your mental health, your physical health might be hurt, too. Pessimism, even though it might be useful when in moderation or isolation, has been associated with heart disease, high blood pressure, hostility, sleep disorders, depression, and anxiety.

## Handling Pessimism

Having expectations that are realistic instead of taking extreme negative or positive positions might be the best recipe for happiness and good health. It might not be surprising but having low levels of pessimism instead of high levels of optimism, have been associated with better health.

This means that pessimism might be one more risk factor for heart disease and other mental and physical health problems; however, being overly optimistic isn't going to prevent you from getting sick. Instead of constantly having a sunny disposition and a bright smile, or giving a negative outlook on life, your goal needs to be moderate optimism with a small dose of pessimism.

### Can a Person Catch Pessimism?

Just like other negative feelings, pessimism could be

144

spread from person to person if they spend enough time together. It might be extremely hard for romantic partners or family to stay away from catching cynical outlooks. A few factors that might make someone more susceptible to "catching" pessimism include their stress levels, personal history, genetics, and other factors.

## Can Pessimism be a Good Thing?

Pessimists can make better leaders, especially if there is a need to create some social change. Their skepticism might make them resist false advertising and propaganda. Defensive pessimism can be useful as a cognitive strategy for many people. They start by setting their expectations low, and then they outperform themselves by being prepared for multiple negative outcomes.

I don't believe in the idea that we have to be smiling and totally happy every minute of every day. And

145

there may be times when a pessimistic view may be valuable. Pessimism might keep you guarded against making some mistakes. It might give you a full picture of any situation rather than being gullible. However, it's role should be a supporting role and not leading. If you allow it to call all the shots, it is going to say "no" to everything. There isn't anything more limiting than that.

To learn about pessimism, you should know about optimism, too.

## What Is Optimism?

*"A pessimist sees the difficulty in every opportunity; an optimist sees the opportunity in every difficulty."*
- Winston Churchill

For psychologists, optimism shows that we believe that the outcome of most experiences or events will be positive. Others believe that optimism is a style;

it lives in how people perceive events. Optimists typically see any negative experiences or failures as only temporary and aren't permanent. This type of perspective supports a Growth Mindset, which promotes the development and growth of the individual.

## What Does It Mean to Be An Optimist

Optimism doesn't mean you engage in fantastic or wishful thinking. It is a way to look at the world that gives you more influence to change your perspective when life isn't going so great. Optimists will have healthier outlooks, and research has shown that they tend to live longer than pessimists. They aren't as susceptible to depression, fatigue, and illness. However, an unrealistic belief that your future will be full of only positive things could lead them to take some unnecessary risks, especially with their finances and health.

## **Tips to Help You Think Positively**

The best habit you can create is to stop being pessimistic and to think in more constructive ways. It can make you feel lighter. You won't feel burdened down. It can open new paths to all the places you want to go to, and it can help you overcome any setbacks you might have. You won't be as worried all the time. You will stop feeling sorry for yourself. You will feel more motivated to take any actions that are needed.

The benefits of being optimistic are great. How can you create this habit? It will help if you begin to think more positively and stop thinking so skeptically.

Here are ten tips that you can begin using right now to help on on your journey:

- Replace the Negative Things in Your Life

All the things that you allow to seep into your mind during your day can have a massive effect on the way you think and feel. You have to begin questioning everything that you allow into your mind. You can do this by asking:

"What are the three biggest negative things in my life?"

It might be someone you see daily at school or work. It might be a website that you visit daily. It could be the music you listen to, a podcast, a television show, or a magazine.

Once you have figured out what these things are, find a piece of paper and ask yourself:

"What can I do to spend less time with these three sources this week?"

Now figure out some ideas and some steps you can

149

do to accomplish this. Now, in the next week, spend the time you have freed up on the positive sources or people that are in your life.

- Find All the Good in Every Negative Situation

The main difference between a pessimist and an optimist is the way that person looks at an obstacle or setback in your life. Anytime I stumbled upon a negative situation, I would just give up and go home. I felt like I was stuck in a permanent place, and it wouldn't matter what I tried. Nothing would make any difference. So my mind would get filled up with pessimistic thoughts, and I would beat myself up for all the things I had done.

I look at things a lot differently now. When I am in a negative situation, I ask myself questions that help to empower me.

Here are some questions you can ask:

- "What is one thing I could do differently the next time to have a better outcome?"
- "What is one thing I could learn from this experience?"
- "What is one good thing about this situation?"
- "How would my parent or best friend help and support me in this situation?"

- Stop Making a Big Deal When There Isn't One

I used to do this all the time. I would blow up the tiniest things into huge monsters. This isn't a great habit if you want to move forward, or you don't want to have a lot of fears or worries in your life.

The easiest way to get yourself grounded in any

situation, where you begin to feel like you might be making a big deal out of nothing, is to take a few minutes and ask yourself these questions:

- ○ "Is this going to matter in five minutes?"
- ○ "Is this going to matter if five weeks?"
- ○ "Is this going to matter in five years?"

It might surprise you to know the answer to all of those is, no, it won't.

- Let It Go

If you allow negative things to bounce around in your mind, they will drag you down. To help you let it go, talk about the negative situation with someone you trust. Venting can help you find a better perspective on the situation. While the other person listens to you, you can take the time to figure out what you would like to do.

152

You might want some more active help. If you both talk about the problem, then you can work together to find a better solution and maybe begin an action plan for all the things you want to make better.

- Take It Slow

If you start going too fast while moving, talking, or even thinking, things won't go too well. Stress can build up, and it will be harder for you to think clearly. Negative thoughts begin to cloud your mind, and it will be hard to stop them. If you can slow your mind, then your body will calm down, too. It will get easier to find an optimistic perspective and constructive ways to get what you want.

- Positively Begin Your Day

The things you do when you wake up can set the tone for your entire day. If you get off to a pessimistic or negative start, then it might be hard

153

to shake these feelings. If you positively start your morning, then it will be a lot easier to remain in that emotional state until it is time to go to bed.

Try placing a reminder on your bathroom mirror or bedside table. It might be a quote that inspires you. It could be something that you are dreaming about getting right now. Write whatever it is on a piece of paper and put it where you will be able to see it in the first few minutes after you get up.

For additional strategies on how to become a more positive thinker, I recommend reading my book Develop a Positive Mindset and Attract the Life of Your Dreams: Unleash Positive Thinking to Achieve Unbound Happiness, Health, and Success.

## **Recap**

Pessimism causes you to see everything in a negative light, which causes you to feel down all of the time. Start trying to look at things in a more positive and optimistic light. Research has shown that keeping a positive attitude and an optimistic outlook has benefits for your overall health and wellbeing.

# Chapter 7: Developing Awareness of Thoughts and Emotions

Tom is a lighting designer at an architecture firm. If you were to ask him if his emotions impact his work, he would laugh in your face. He would tell you that the only thing that matters is being able to turn his client's vision into a design that is aesthetically pleasing and practical. Feelings don't have anything to do with his designs.

Now, ask Tom's coworkers, and you are going to hear a different story. They will tell you that how he works with his coworkers and clients is inconsistent. All will go well when he is in a good mood. His interactions will suffer if he is frustrated or angry. He will show contempt for a suggestion made by a client, plus he won't listen to them. Most of his clients reject his first design because he didn't do what they wanted. His coworkers know that if he is in a bad mood, to stay away from him.

Tom's failure to understand his feelings and the way they can influence his behavior can hurt his work performance. He doesn't have emotional self-awareness.

## Emotional Self-Awareness

Emotional self-awareness is being able to understand and recognize emotions and the way they can impact your behavior. You should know the way you feel and why you are feeling like that. You should be able to see how these feelings either hurt or help the things you do. You will also have a good sense of the way others see you. Emotional self-

158

awareness is different from cognitive self-awareness, which focuses on your ideas and thoughts rather than your feelings.

## Developing Self-Awareness

Being able to see your feelings and how they influence your actions is a skill that you can develop, just like learning how to play tennis or swim. Just like there are different levels to these skills, noticing feelings isn't something that you do one time and then you have it for the rest of your life. It takes practice and attention to develop. Then you have to maintain by doing it each day, just like practicing mindfulness.

The primary tool for developing your self-awareness is by tuning into your body. If you feel angry or scared, your heart will start pounding faster than when you feel calm. You may start breathing faster and begin sweating. The muscles in your shoulders might tighten up.

Our brains have a map of our bodies. The insula has specific cells that relate to various organs throughout the body. Cell groups in the insula have been tuned into our lungs, heart, and other organs. Interoception is the capacity to sense muscle tension, heart rate, and other signals from the body. The insula will then pass along the signals it gets from our body to the brain. The brain then decides how important the signal is and what it needs to do with this information.

## **Steps You Can Take to Develop Your Thoughts and Feelings**

You know that your thoughts are just an inner dialogue. An average person can have around 6000 thoughts per day, most of these you repeat over and over again. They have essentially become a habit. Many of these thoughts come from the experiences you had from childhood, and you have repeated them ever since.

Why do you need to develop your awareness of these thoughts? Being able to choose the way you think about yourself and your life around you lets you respond, control, and regulate any event that triggers you.

You need to be aware of all the things you tell yourself so you can direct your choices. If you want to be happy, you have to do this. This is crucial since your thoughts can activate processes that are driven by emotions inside you. Yes, even the painful ones. Thoughts, along with your underlying beliefs, can trigger your emotions.

Even though people's actions and events might trigger some unpleasant reactions and feelings, they aren't the cause of them. The activating agents are the things you tell yourself. Most of the things you

161

tell yourself you do on a subconscious level. This comes from all the beliefs that you hold close to you, and most of these operate on a subconscious level.

When you, and not your emotions, are in control of the things you think, you will be in charge of your behavior. This, in turn, gives you more power over the way events will unfold in your life. Developing your self-awareness is the first thing you need to do to start changing your thoughts.

## How to Develop Your Emotional Self-Awareness

Here are some steps you can use to help you learn to be aware of your feelings and how they connect to your thoughts.

1. Choose a Situation to Process

Write down a list of events that triggers anger or

upsets you. Now choose one that isn't too challenging to work on. With some time and practice, you can take on more and more triggers. You need to work your way up to the more challenging ones gradually. This might take you days, weeks, or even months. You are going to need to be patient. You will have to move out of your comfort zones but don't overwhelm yourself in the process. If at any time, this gets too intense, stop working on this by yourself. If this happens, you might need to find a therapist or counselor who can help you.

- Ground Yourself in The Present

After choosing the trigger that you want to work on, take a few minutes and take three to five deep breaths, to center yourself. Breathe in deep from the belly and relax your body. Exhale through your mouth and focus. Close your eyes, and focus on your breath, scan your body from your head down to your toes for tension. If you find any, notice it, and then release all tightness and tension.

Visualize yourself inside a safe place. Remember that you aren't your thoughts or emotions. You are the choice maker, creator, and observer of your thoughts and emotions. Remind yourself that this is good. This means you have complete control over how you respond. Nobody can "make you" feel anything without you giving your permission. You are observing your emotions. Notice any emotions that you are experiencing as being old energy pockets. They are old childhood wounds that don't mean anything now. They come from a time when you didn't know how to look at your life from a different perspective. You are now a capable and intelligent adult who is in charge of your mental processes. You get to choose when to stop this exercise. You can stop at any time you need to.

- Feel and Recognize Your Feelings and Emotions

While you are feeling centered and relaxed with your breathing, bring the trigger you selected to mind. Try to recall when it happened recently. Don't judge but pause and be aware of your sensations and feelings. If you feel angry, try to find the emotions behind it. These emotions can be a bit overwhelming. You need to ask yourself: "What is lying under this anger?"

What emotions and feelings are you feeling? Jot these down on a piece of paper or in your journal.

- Notice and Feel Any Sensations

Take a moment and allow yourself to feel every emotion and notice what sensation you feel. For every one of the emotions that got triggered, figure out what sensations you feel when you see the

165

event that triggered this emotion. Notice and observe where these sensations are located. Feel these sensations, breathe into them deeply. Gently place either one or both hands on the place you feel them. While you are doing this, let go of any impulses you have to stop, judge, suppress, or fix these sensations or emotions. Continue exploring and notice if the sensations lessen. If anger is the primary sensation, keep asking yourself: "What else am I feeling?"

Try to describe the sensations you felt in your body. In a column next to the emotions you listed earlier, write down all the sensations you are feeling and where you felt them.

- Accept Your Feelings

Keep telling yourself that you and your emotions are two different things. You are only observing your emotions. Emotions and energy are the same things.

All the things you are feeling are just pockets of supercharged energy that are linked to wounds from your past. Since you are the ruler of your life, you get to choose to breathe into any energy that feels painful, notice if it changes, move, and then release it. You get to decide if you want to affirm the power that you possess as a ruler to accept any painful feelings as being natural due to the circumstance that you are telling yourself. Confidently and calmly affirm: "I accept what I am feeling in this very moment."

Say this either silently or out loud. Out loud would be better: "I can handle this emotion... I am strong and able to handle this calmly, easily, and wisely."

- Recognize the Things You Tell Yourself That Trigger Painful Emotions

Now, you need to notice the thoughts you think when you visualize the event that triggered your emotions. Try to find any toxic patterns. Your thought can trigger physical sensations and emotions in your body. This is how the brain works.

Observe these thoughts from a distance that is safe and where you are objective. You are just noticing and not judging. Use this visual anytime a disturbing thought comes up. Visualize yourself on a speeding train. You are looking out your window and see all your upsetting thoughts zip by you while you are sitting inside your train car, safe and sound.

Write down anything additional that you tell yourself besides the sensations and emotions that you have already written down.

## Recap

Awareness of your emotions and thoughts is 90% of the solution. Once you are away from your emotions, then you can start to heal and form a more positive thought process. Start noticing your emotional triggers and then look at those triggers to see if they are exaggerated or biased from your perception. You will likely find most of your emotional responses to things are somewhat over-the-top. Take advantage of the strategies discussed, and move towards developing a healthy mind and emotionally self-aware.

# CHAPTER 8: REPROGRAMMING YOUR MIND

Our brains are constantly evolving based on our experiences. Many of us have different beliefs and behaviors now than we did ten years ago. This is due to neuroplasticity. Neuroplasticity is any change in our brain's organization and structure while we learn how to adapt, learn, and experience.

With every repetitive emotion or thought, we are reinforcing a neural pathway. With every new idea, we start creating a new way of living. These little changes, if repeated enough, can lead to changes in the way our brain works.

The things we do the most get stronger and the things we don't use will eventually fade away. This is the basis of why doing an action or having a thought continuously will increase its power. With time, it will automatically become a part of you. You become what you think and do.

You have to work on rewiring your brain. The brain's connections are getting either weaker or stronger, depending on what you are doing. Younger people find it easier to change because their brains are extremely plastic. However, as we get older, we don't change as quickly. The brain loses some of its plasticity, and we get more fixed in the way we perceive, learn, and think.

## Reticular Activating System

The Reticular Activating System (RAS) is a bundle of nerves that sits at our brainstem that can filter out any information that isn't needed, so all the essential

172

things get through. This system is the reason we can learn a new word and then hear it everywhere you go. This is why you can tune out a crowd of people talking but come back to reality when somebody says our name or something similar to it.

The Reticular Activating System sifts through all the data and gives you the critical pieces. This happens without you even realizing it. This system programs itself to work to your advantage without you actually doing anything.

It will look for information that will validate your beliefs. It can filter your world through any parameter you choose to give it. What you believe can shape these parameters. If you think you're bad at talking in front of people, you will be. If you think you work efficiently, you probably will. The RAS can help you see all the things you want to see, and this, in turn, can influence your actions.

There is a belief that you can train your RAS by taking subconscious thoughts and bringing them into your conscious thoughts. This is called "setting your intent." This means if you focus on your goals, your RAS will show you the opportunities, information, and people that can help you reach your goals.

If you set an intention to be more positive and focus on it, you will be more aware and will seek positivity. If you want a pet and you set an intention on getting one, you will find the right information that will lead you to one.

If you focus on bad things, then you are inviting negativity into your life. Focus on all the good things, and they will find you since your brain has been looking for them. It isn't magic; it is your RAS influencing the world as you see it.

Without clear goals, our RAS is similar to a confused

174

personal assistant with no clear instructions from the Boss – you. It will benefit you to create a list of the things you want and read it often. You have to refocus your brain on the things that matter and away from the things that don't.

## Emotional Intelligence

Politics, relationships, money, and job pressure; these are just some of the leading causes of stress. This is something that everyone experiences, and it can affect our mental health. We don't have control over all the things that cause us stress, but we can be more aware of our stress indicators and ways we can start managing our stress better. It begins with improving emotional intelligence.

We have heard for years about how we need to see things from other people's perspectives or to have empathy toward others. This can be hard if you aren't aware of your own stressors and ways to

175

regulate yourself. Improving your emotional intelligence can help you handle your stress, empathize with others, building stronger relationships, and reaching your goals. At work, you will be able to assess and change relationships and situations better, cope with stress, demands, and pressures, and negotiate and navigate conflict.

Emotional intelligence can affect the way we relate to others, and this includes the way we lead and manage. If we want to improve our emotional intelligence, we have to know all of its components:

- Self-Awareness

You need to be aware of all the different aspects of yourself, and this includes your feelings and emotions. A self-aware person will be able to understand their emotions while not allowing their feelings to control them. They will be confident, willing to honestly look at themselves, and know all

176

their weaknesses and strengths.

- Self-Regulation

You need to be able to control your impulses and emotions. People who can regulate themselves usually don't allow themselves to get jealous or angry. They won't make careless or impulsive decisions. They take the time to think before they act.

- Empathy and Social Skills

You need to be aware of other people's emotions. A person who has a high emotional intelligence will be a team player, excellent communicator, good listener, skilled in maintaining and creating relationships, able to manage conflicts efficiently, and recognize other people's feelings.

- Motivation

177

We all have aspirations, no matter how big or small they may be. You need to be optimistic and committed. A person who has high emotional intelligence will have the drive to achieve, improve, take initiatives, and will be ready to handle all challenges.

## Cognitive Behavioral Therapy

Another effective method to reprogram your mind is the use of Cognitive Behavioral Therapy or CBT. This is a short-term, goal-oriented psychotherapy treatment. It has a practical and hands-on approach to problem-solving. Many people will start doing CBT with a psychologist, but there are techniques that you can learn that doesn't require a psychologist. The following are some easy methods that you can try.

## Mindfulness

Mindfulness is something that can help to cool off any unwanted or unhealthy negative emotions, including anger. Let's see mindfulness at work, and how it can help. You get home to find that your partner hasn't done anything you have asked them to do. You were working late, you are stressed, and you can feel the anger starting to rise within you. Logically, you know it would be better to talk things through, but that can be hard when you're upset. You can stop and do the following.

1. Became aware of the negative emotion in your body. Notice the physical sensations in your face, stomach, and chest. Notice your rapid heartbeat and how fast you are breathing. Notice if your jaw or fists are clenched.

2. Next, take a deep breath and breathe into those physical sensations. Close your eyes at this point, if you would like. Counting to ten as you breathe in might be helpful. See the breath as it enters your nose, moves into your belly, and then as it moves back out your mouth as you release the breath.

3. Continue to stay with these sensations for as long as possible. Bring in the sense of gentleness to your feelings. Try to see this negative moment as a chance to understand more about your feelings.

4. Notice any thoughts you may be having. Notice how it feels to let go of any of these negative thoughts. If you can't let them go, which is common, continue to watch how your feelings and thoughts are feeding each other.

5. Take a step back from your internal situation. Notice how you are observing your emotions and thoughts and that you aren't the emotions or thoughts themselves.

6. As soon as the initial force of the negativity has left, you can continue by communicating how you feel. Make sure you use "I" statements and not "you" statements.

The important part of mindfulness is that you notice things for what they are and take a step back from the heat of the moment. You can also do a simple mindfulness meditation at the end of the day. It would follow the same steps as above, except you might not have a negative emotion that you need to wash away.

**Half-Smile Technique**

For this technique, you are going to need ten

undisturbed minutes. Make sure that you are relaxed and comfortable. This exercise is meant to create an environment where serenity can grow and be enhanced. The muscles in the face send signals and messages to the brain and vice versa. Emotions have a strong relationship with your facial muscles, as well. Just think about the fact that you smile when happy, frown when you're mad, and many other expressions.

This half-smile is a soft, almost imperceptible smile. The half-smile begins with relaxed lips, which you turn slightly upward and a loose jaw. Make sure your eyes are relaxed and soft. Then the half-smile will spread to the entire face as the neck and scalp relax, and your shoulders drop. You can close your eyes at this point and just sit with your breath and the serenity. You may find it helpful to visualize some things that evoke serenity. Once your ten minutes are up, find a way to remember that serenity you found at that moment. Practice this regularly.

**Square Breathing**

This is a type of breathwork that helps to shift your energy, connect you to your body, decrease stress, and calm your nervous system. It is sometimes called box breathing, 4-part breath, and 4x4 breathing.

If you can, sit in a chair with your back supported and feet on the floor. You can also do this in a seated meditation pose, or laying down. The main this is to make sure that your body is opened so that you can breathe freely.

1. Start by slowly exhaling all of your breath out.
2. Gently breathe in through your nose to a count of four.
3. Hold the breath for another count of four.
4. Then slowly release your breath through your mouth for another four counts.

5. Hold your breath at the bottom of the breath for a count of four.

The great thing about this breath is that you can do it anywhere and at any time. Whenever you start feeling stressed or upset, you can take the time to practice square breathing to calm yourself down.

**Progressive Muscle Relaxation**

This is a relaxation technique that helps to relieve tension. With this exercise, you tense a muscle group as you take a breath in and then relax the muscles as you release your breath. As you do this, you are unable to feel anxious. The more you do this, the easier it will be for you to reduce your stress using the method. When you do this the first few times, you might find it helpful to find an audio of PMR on YouTube. It will help you to focus on the actual muscles rather than thinking about what you are supposed to be doing.

184

Start by laying down and relaxing a bit into the soft surface. On your next breath in, clench your hands and hold for a few seconds. Release your breath and hands completely. Take about 10 seconds before continuing to the next muscle group. You should take these 10 seconds after each muscle group.

When you breathe in again, tense your wrists and forearms by bending the hands back towards the arm. Hold for a few seconds, and then release the muscles completely as you breathe out. Continue this process with the rest of the muscle groups as follows.

- Biceps and upper arms – clench your hands and then bend your arms at the elbows to flex your biceps.
- Shoulders – shrug them
- Forehead – frown
- Around the eyes and nose – close your eyes tightly.

185

- Jaws and cheeks – smile as wide as you can
- The mouth – press your lips together
- Back of neck – press your head back against what you're laying on
- Font of the neck – touch your chin to your chest
- Chest – take a very deep breath
- Back – arch your back up
- Stomach – suck in your stomach
- Hips and buttocks – squeeze your buttocks tightly
- Thighs – clench them
- Lower legs – point your toes towards your face and then point them away, and then curl them down

**Visualization**

Entrepreneurs, top athletes, and highly driven people use visualization. It has been found that people who envision themselves performing a particular task prior to execution tend to improve their performance in the task. Practicing visualization in the morning will help you to connect your emotions with your long-term and short-term goals. Through visualization, you can change your mindset and get closer to what you want.

1.  Figure out what you want.

The first thing you need to do is have a clear idea as to what it is that you would like to do and why. To figure this out, answer this question, If I had nothing preventing me from doing this, what would I want to have in my life?

2.  Describe this vision in detail.

This is the most important thing. You need to have a clear vision of what it is that your life will look like. You can do this by writing it down or making a vision board.

187

3.  Start to visualize and form emotions.

Once you know what you want and how it looks, take some time to start envisioning the outcome. Start to think about the smells, sounds, sights, and taste of achieving the things that you want. Don't forget to feel all of the emotions connected to that moment.

4.  Take daily action steps.

The only way you are going to get what you visualized is if you do something to bring it to you. It's not enough just to think about it. You have to put legs on those dreams and work on it daily.

**Reframing Negative Thoughts**

We can fall into a bunch of thinking traps due to our perception of events. This causes us to think things are worse than they are, but we have tools to stop that. Try reframing when you start to feel that a situation is helpless and beyond your control. Reframing will remove the negativity in the situation and will empower you to change the meaning that you assign to the experience into something positive.

Here's how - Recognize that the intrusive thought has taken over. Be intentional about stopping the thought. Replace it with something happy. Ask yourself questions such as: What other meaning could this event have? In what ways could this prove to be a resource or a positive experience?

If you are magnifying, which means you jump to unjustified conclusions, you overgeneralize. To reframe, focus on the big picture. Move on and know that you have the power to do better and change.

If you are thinking in means of black and white, you

189

think it has to be right or has to be wrong, and you are setting yourself up for failure. To reframe, give yourself some slack. Nobody is perfect, and the world is full of gray areas. You need to be flexible and go with the flow.

If you think that everything that happens has something to do with you, you are hurting yourself because you are blaming yourself for things you had no control over. To reframe this, realize that just because something is occurring near you doesn't mean it has anything to do with you. You are not the center of the universe.

**Affirmations**

Affirmations or mantras are great ways to build up self-belief within the subconscious mind. They can help to inspire you and motivate you to be better and overcome any barriers you may have. When you first start to say your affirmation, they may not

190

be true, but they will resonate in your mind so that you are motivated to make them true.

You can say your affirmation at any time during the day, but making sure you say it first thing in the morning is best. This will set a positive mood for the day. It is best if you come up with your own affirmations, but here are a few options.

- "I am releasing all of my negative beliefs I have about money."
- "My life is full of love and joy."
- "I respect and love myself."
- "My mind is bursting with bright ideas, kind words, and happiness."
- "The only approval I need is my own."

**The Table Leg Method**

This method helps you to change your long-held beliefs. You do this by imagining that your belief is like a tabletop and the evidence that supports the belief is in the legs. You look at this evidence and conclude. Much like a table, if you were to knock enough of those legs out, the belief is going to collapse. This is done by creating doubt about the evidence you have or looking at things differently. Once you bust down that old belief that has been holding you back, you can build a new, healthy belief in the same way.

1. Find your limiting belief that you want to get rid of. List out all of the things that provide this belief support. Make sure you have at least three pieces of evidence.

2. Find a different belief that is more empowering. This could just be the exact opposite of the old belief, or something new. Make sure that you can believe the idea and that it will be an improved belief.

3. Get rid of the emotional glue. We can get attacked by these limiting beliefs, but an excellent way to get rid of the glue is to ask what this belief is doing for you if you hold on to it.

4. Reframe your evidence by creating doubt. For each piece of evidence, ask these questions. "What is another explanation?" "Is there more to this?" "Could it be untrue?" You want to create doubt.

5. Find evidence that supports a healthy belief. Flip everything around and build up supporting evidence to help solidify your brand new healthy belief. You need a minimum of three pieces of evidence. With enough legs, your new belief will stand strong.

You can now get rid of destructive beliefs and build

up healthy ones.

## Recap

Increasing your emotional intelligence is the best way to improve your happiness and reduce your negativity. Look back through the CBT techniques and choose one that resonates with you the most and gives it a try. If you find that it doesn't work that well for you, then pick a different technique. You do not have to use all of them. You may find one work really well or that there are a couple of the techniques that work for you. The important thing is to do what can help you feel better.

# CHAPTER 9: THE POWER OF GRATITUDE

We all would like to be able to take a magic pill that would fix all of our problems. It would make us more productive, optimistic, healthy, and happier. You would want that pill, wouldn't you?

Unfortunately, I don't have a pill that I could give you, but I have something even better that can do those things and more. It's called gratitude. Science has proven that an "attitude of gratitude" is a healthy choice. When you are more grateful, it will make you more optimistic and happier. Gratitude also adds to the bottom line. The best thing about gratitude is

**195**

that it doesn't require any money.

The law of attraction explains that we attract into our lives the things that we focus on and think about. Doesn't that mean we would want to be more thankful? Whenever you are consciously aware of the good things in your life and are grateful for those things, you focus more clearly on the things that you want in life, and you will attract more of those things.

## **Gratitude Helps Your Relationships**

As children, we learn that we should say thank you. We are taught that this is good manners. This is a childhood lesson that we need to remember into adulthood. Think about all of those people that you know who are appreciative of you, and they let you know it. What are your feelings towards them? Does the way they feel about you impact your relationship with them? I'm sure it does. Make sure you let them know you are grateful for having them in your lives and also show gratitude to all those who contribute to your life, and make sure you tell them how you feel.

## **Gratitude Gets Rid of Negativity**

It's pretty hard to feel negatively towards a situation when you think about things that you are grateful for. The quickest way to improve your mood is to think about all of the things you have.

We often look at our problems in a very jaded light. When something goes wrong, we create barriers in our way. Then we have to use more effort to fix the issue. Conversely, if we think about what we are most grateful for, we open up the mind to new connections and possibilities. We will be able to enter into a problem-solving situation with a perspective of opportunity and improvement rather than an issue or challenge.

197

All clouds have a silver lining. Behind all of our problems is an opportunity. When you are grateful in a situation, even if you don't like everything about it, it gives you the chance to be thankful for the opportunity to learn something new.

### But How Can I Be Grateful?

At this point, you're probably thinking, "Alright, sounds great, but how can I be more grateful?" It's actually one of the easiest things you can do in life. Let's take a moment to practice some gratitude.

1.  Create a list of five things that you are thankful for right now. You can make these things as big or as small as you would like them to be. You can do this mentally or write it down.

2. Once you have your list, reflect on it, and allow yourself to feel good about all of those things.

3. If there is a person on your list that you can thank or show some appreciation for, then do it right now.

This exercise can be done at any time, and you don't have to stick with five items. It is a good idea to keep a running list in a notebook or journals. This way, you will have something to look back on whenever you want to reinforce your gratitude.

At any moment during the day, you can make a list, bask in that feeling, and share thankfulness with other people. You may have had the thought that being thankful is the "right" thing to do, but hopefully, you will see that being grateful can be more powerful than right.

Gratitude should be a habit. When we consciously practice the act of gratefulness for people, resources, or situations we have, we start to attract better results and relationships. The habit is going to strengthen as you choose to practice it every day.

## **Recap**

Gratitude is one of the best ways to bring happiness into your life. Even when you are having one horrible day after the next, take a moment to stop and think about all of the things you are grateful for. Do you have a home to live in? Do you have money for food? Do you have a person who cares about you? All of those things, and more, are reasons to be grateful.

# CONCLUSION

Thank you for making it through to the end of the book; let's hope it was informative and able to provide you with all of the tools you need to achieve your goals to become a happier person in charge of your emotions.

In life, we have ups and downs, and we have to learn how to ride them with grace. This can be tough because sometimes you have days where it would just be easier to crawl back into bed and pretend like the world doesn't exist. We can't do that either. What we can do is tap into the power of our minds and relearn how to be happy and more positive. We can learn how to find the silver lining in the darkest of clouds so that we can work through the bad and get to the good. We don't have to feel like we are trapped in our emotions. Instead, we can choose not to let the world get us down.

We also know that we can't always be positive because then we are verging on the "I'm just kidding myself" line. Bad, sad, and upsetting things will happen. We'll get frustrated and angry, but we will know how to handle those emotions. We won't be at the mercy of these emotions any longer. We can feel them, notice them, and accept them for what they are and then move on. Gone are the days when we have to plaster on a happy face and muddle through because we will know how actually to be positive even if something bad happens.

This book has provided you with the tools that you need to overcome emotional and mental obstacles. It's not a quick-fix tool by any means, and it will

202

require some work, but it can be done with the right mindset. As you start rewiring your brain, you will notice that happiness and positivity come more naturally. You will find that you are more grateful for the smaller things that you may have taken for granted before.

Everybody's journey is going to be different. Some people have more emotional problems that they have to work through before they are on auto-pilot with happiness. Some may have issues with anger, while others are stuck in the world of pessimism. That's okay. The tools you have learned in this book can help no matter what your situation is. The important thing is to make sure you pick what works best for you and be persistent. Listen to your body and mind and learn what you need. Don't worry about anybody else. You are the important one.

All the best in your efforts!

# Thank You!

## Thank you for your purchase.

I am dedicated to making the most enriching and informational content. I hope it meets your expectations and you gain a lot from it.

Your comments and feedback are important to me because they help me to provide the best material possible. So, if you have any questions or concerns, please email me at richardbanks.books@gmail.com.

Again, thank you for your purchase.

**One more thing...**

If you enjoyed this book and found it helpful, I'd be very grateful if you'd post a short review on Amazon. Your support does make a difference, and I read all the reviews personally so I can get your feedback and make this book even better. I love hearing from my readers and I'd really appreciate if you left your honest feedback.

Thank you for reading!

# REFERENCES

*Cognitive Behavioral Therapy*. (n.d.). Psychology Today. Retrieved September 1, 2020, from https://www.psychologytoday.com/us/basics/cognitive-behavioral-therapy

Cousins, L. (2018, February). *Why 'bottling it up' can be harmful to your health | HCF*. Health Agenda. https://www.hcf.com.au/health-agenda/body-mind/mental-health/downsides-to-always-being-positive

Edberg, H. (2020, September 7). *How to Stop Being Pessimistic: 10 Positive Thinking Tips*. The Positivity Blog. https://www.positivityblog.com/positive-thinking/

Goleman, D. (2018, August 15). *How Emotionally Self-Aware Are You?* Mindful. https://www.mindful.org/emotionally-self-aware/

Harvard Health Publishing. (n.d.). *Giving thanks can make you happier*. Harvard Health. Retrieved September 1, 2020, from https://www.health.harvard.edu/healthbeat/giving-thanks-can-make-you-happier

Holland, K. (2019, February 11). *10 Defense Mechanisms: What Are They and How They Help Us Cope*. Healthline. https://www.healthline.com/health/mental-health/defense-mechanisms

Lawson, K. (n.d.). *What Are Thoughts & Emotions?* Taking Charge of Your Health & Wellbeing. Retrieved September 1, 2020, from https://www.takingcharge.csh.umn.edu/what-are-thoughts-emotions

Lewis, R. (2019, February 24). *What Actually Is a Thought? And How Is Information Physical?* Psychology Today. https://www.psychologytoday.com/us/blog/finding-purpose/201902/what-actually-is-thought-and-how-is-information-physical

Maloney, B. (2020, January 22). *The Damaging Effects of Negativity | Marque Medical Blog.* Marque Medical. https://marquemedical.com/damaging-effects-of-negativity/

Marta, G. D. (2014, May 11). *Core beliefs, automatic thoughts and conceptualisation in CBT.* Counselling Directory. https://www.counselling-directory.org.uk/memberarticles/core-beliefs-automatic-thoughts-and-conceptualization-in-cbt

mindbodygreen. (2020, February 25). *What Are Emotional Triggers + Why You Need To Understand Them.* https://www.mindbodygreen.com/0-18348/what-are-emotional-triggers-why-you-need-to-understand-them.html

*Pessimism.* (n.d.). Psychology Today. Retrieved September 1, 2020, from https://www.psychologytoday.com/us/basics/pessimism

Vassar, G. (2011, March 1). *Do You Know Your Anger Triggers?* Lakeside. https://lakesidelink.com/blog/lakeside/do-you-know-your-anger-triggers/

*What Is A Growth Mindset?* (n.d.). Renaissance. Retrieved September 1, 2020, from https://www.renaissance.com/edwords/growth-mindset/

*What is Neuroplasticity? Brain plasticity explained – UK.* (n.d.). BrainWorks. Retrieved September 1, 2020, from https://brainworksneurotherapy.com/what-neuroplasticity

Made in the USA
Monee, IL
16 December 2024

73978979R00125